WHAT DO I WANT IN PRAYER?

WILLIAM A. BARRY, S.J.

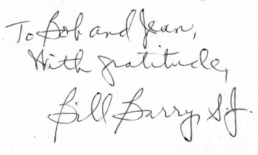

To Bob and Jean,
With gratitude,
Bill Barry, S.J.

PAULIST PRESS
New York, NY • Mahwah, NJ

Excerpts from the Spiritual Exercises are taken from George E. Ganss, *The Spiritual Exercises of St. Ignatius: A Translation and Commentary*, © 1992 by The Institute of Jesuit Sources, St. Louis, MO. The translation of the kingdom meditation was taken from Joseph Tetlow's *Choosing Christ in the World: Directing the Spiritual Exercises of St. Ignatius of Loyola According to Annotations Eighteen and Nineteen*, © 1989 by The Institute of Jesuit Sources, St. Louis, MO. Permission is gratefully acknowledged. Scripture quotations are from the *New Revised Standard Version of the Bible*, copyright 1989 by the Division of Christian Education of the National Council of Churches of Christ in the USA. Used by permission. All rights reserved. Selections from *The Diary of a Country Priest* by Georges Bernanos, translated by Pamela Morris, are copyrighted by The Bodley Head, Ltd, London.

Library of Congress Cataloging-in-Publication Data

Barry William A.
    What do I want in prayer? / by William A. Barry, S.J.
        p.   cm.
    Includes bibliographical references.
    ISBN 0-8091-3482-9 (pbk.)
    1. Prayer—Catholic Church. 2. Spiritual life—Catholic Church. 3. Spiritual exercises. 4. Ignatius, of Loyola, Saint, 1491-1556. Exercitia spiritualia. I. Title.
BV215.B374   1994
248.3—dc20   94-17578
                                                                    CIP

Published by Paulist Press
997 Macarthur Boulevard
Mahwah, NJ 07430

Printed and bound in the
United States of America

TABLE OF CONTENTS

I dedicate this book to spiritual directors, past and present,
who have helped me toward the "pearl of great price"
and to appreciate the *Spiritual Exercises*:
the late John Post, S.J., my novice director
the late William Murphy, S.J., my tertian director
the late William Read, S.J.
Paul T. Lucey, S.J.
Joseph E. McCormick, S.J.
Anne Harvey, S.N.D.

PREFACE

For many years I have been directing individuals through the *Spiritual Exercises* of St. Ignatius of Loyola, the founder of the Society of Jesus. I have become convinced that the key for directing individuals is to know their desires. If they know what they want of the Lord, then I can suggest some exercises for them that give God a chance to fulfill their desires.

As I see it, the development of any relationship is fueled by the desire of each of the persons to know more about the other. In the course of the development of the relationship the desires shift, go deeper, change. But no matter how they change, they still remain desires for more self-revelation on the part of the other. At first, I may just be interested in seeing if you might become a friend. My desire is to get to know you better. If our relationship develops, I will want to know what you think of me, what your values are, whom and what you like and dislike. Even though I seem to desire something different as time goes on, I still want you to reveal something about yourself. The development of the relationship with God is similar. Its beginning depends on my desire to know something about God. In the gospel of John, Jesus noticed two disciples of John the Baptist following him. He asked them, "What are you looking for?" They replied, "Rabbi, where are you staying?" Not a strong desire, but a desire nevertheless. Jesus responds, "Come and see" (Jn 1: 38–39). Their desire led them on a journey they could never have predicted when they showed curiosity about this man pointed out by John the Baptist. Often enough I have people use this passage at the beginning of a retreat so that they can find out what they want at this time of their developing relationship with God.

Throughout the English-speaking world one can sense a hunger for meaning growing. Scott Peck's *The Road Less Traveled* has been on the *New York Times'* Best Seller list for over 500 weeks. That's almost ten years. This is only one example of how a book that helps people to discover meaning in their lives attracts readers. This hunger for meaning translates for many people into a hunger for God. As a result books on prayer are a hot item in religious book stores. The fact that you have this book in your hands shows that you have at least a bit of that hunger. In addition, retreat houses that are known to be helpful to people's prayer life are often overbooked. Many such houses give the *Spiritual Exercises* of St. Ignatius of Loyola in a way tailored to the individual retreatant. Good spiritual directors, i.e., those who gain a deserved reputation for helping individuals with their prayer, find themselves inundated with requests for help. However, many people cannot go to a retreat house or find a good spiritual director. How can they slake their hunger for God? How can they develop their relationship with God?

Over the past few years I have written a few books about prayer as a personal relationship and about the *Spiritual Exercises*. Recently, Paulist Press published a book on my approach to directing the Exercises (*Allowing the Creator to Deal with the Creature*). In a letter accepting the manuscript for publication Don Brophy said that Paulist would like "to publish something fresh on prayer—maybe something on 'desire.' You note in these pages that identifying one's desire has become something of a *lingua franca* in seekers.

Maybe a popular book with an Ignatian-scriptural foundation could make the process more intentional." As it turned out, I was about to prepare to give a guided retreat to about forty members of my province of the Jesuits. In a guided retreat the director gives two talks a day to guide the retreatants' prayer for the day. As I reflected on an approach, it occurred to me that I might begin to work out a book along the lines suggested by Don Brophy. What you have in your hands is the result. I hope that it will be helpful to those people who have a hunger for God and who want to approach the satisfaction of that hunger in a somewhat systematic way.

After an introductory chapter which is descriptive of the process suggested in the book, I use as the title of each chapter a rather specific desire. My intent is to help you, the reader, to identify your desire at any particular time in the development of your relationship with God. I then suggest some exercises for you to do that may give God a chance to fulfill your desire. What I have done is to ransack my memory to see what desires have surfaced in retreatants and what exercises I have suggested to them that seemed to help. I offer these suggestions to you.

It is very important that you recognize your real desires. If you are terribly afraid of God, you will never be able to ask God to reveal to you how God sees you. At this time your real desire is probably to know that God is not so terrifying. Take very seriously the title of the chapter and ask yourself if you really do, at least a little bit, desire what the title says.

I have also designed the book so that you can make your "retreat" any place without having to carry a parcel of books around with you. I have included almost all the scripture texts I suggest for periods of prayer. Thus, you could take this little book with you to work and use part of your lunch hour as a prayer period. You could carry it around wherever you go and use it when you have some free time. There is a growing movement for people to make Ignatian retreats in daily life. They spend some time in prayer each day or in some other regular way. If they can see a director, they share with the director what happens in these periods of prayer and then get direction for the next period of prayer. I have designed this book for those who want to do something like that, but may not have the luxury of being able to see a director very often, if at all. The book can also be used by someone who can get away for some extended time of prayer either alone or with others but cannot do so at a retreat house where a director is available. I hope that the ways this book can be used will depend on the ingenuity of those who pick it up and feel that it might help them to pray and to come to know God better.

I want to thank Don Brophy for the suggestion that resulted in this book. I also want to thank Marika Geoghegan, Bill Russell, S.J. and Bill Devine, S.J. who read the original manuscript and encouraged me to continue to work on it. I am immensely grateful to all those men and women who have trusted me with their hunger for God and the experiences of the encounter with God that satisfied their hunger. I have dedicated the book to my past and present spiritual directors, all of whom have helped me to understand the movements of the Spiritual Exercises and to satisfy my hunger for God and especially have helped me to recognize the deepest desire of my heart when I had let other attachments and my fear get in the way.

I commend the exercises in this book to you. I hope that you will find the "pearl of great price" and sell all to acquire it. I also recommend that you use the suggestions that help you and forget the ones that do not help. Because, for example, St. Ignatius suggests ending each period of prayer with an Our Father, you are not required

to do so slavishly even if saying the Our Father is more of a
hindrance than a help to your prayer. May the good God
bless you abundantly and draw you into closer intimacy in
accordance with your desires.

1

INTRODUCTORY NOTES
ABOUT YOUR RETREAT

The word "retreat" may put you off. A retreat in battle
signals defeat. The word summons up images of bedrag-
gled and disheartened people slinking away, hoping to get
out of it with their bones intact. For the more religiously
inclined the word "retreat" conjures up images of monks
and nuns walking around singly, in silence, their eyes
focused on the ground, and looking rather grim. "Retreat
means days in silence and prayer; how can I manage it? I'm
not a monk or nun; I'm not holy." The fact that you have
this book in your hands indicates one thing, namely, that
you are intrigued by the idea of developing your relationship time with God. Try to think of your "retreat" as time
with someone who loves you very much and whom you
would like to know better. If you are able to take some time
off for this retreat, think of it as a vacation with the Lord,
a chance to get to know God and Jesus better and to let
them know you better. If you are only able to take some
time for prayer each day or periodically during a week, you
can still think of that time as put aside for developing your
relationship with the Lord. Prayer is, after all is said and
done, a rather simple thing: it is conscious relationship.

The old Baltimore Catechism defined prayer as the rais-
ing of the mind and heart to God. That means conscious
relationship. I pay attention to God, to my own desires for

God, to the hints in my experience that God is communicating with me. In my small book *God and You* I develop at length this definition of prayer as conscious relationship. Here let's focus for a moment on the analogy of the development of a human relationship. How do you get to know another person? First, you have to be interested in that person, to be attracted to her. You will not be tempted to spend time with another person if you are not in some way interested in her. Then, given the initial interest, you take some initiative to be with her, to get to know her. At first, the attempts may just be exploratory; you may begin talking about the weather or some other topic that will start the ball rolling. But if the relationship is to get off the ground, you will want to know something about her, and you hope that she will want to know something about you. Relationships develop through mutual self-revelation. In the beginning these self-revelations tend to be rather superficial. "Where do you come from?" "Where did you go to school?" These are the kinds of questions that elicit information about the other. Eventually, of course, if both of you want to deepen the relationship, you will want to know more about one another's heart; not only "Where did you go to school?" but also "How did you like it there? What happened to you there?" You will want to know how each of you feels about the other; you will begin to communicate to one another about your reactions to one another. The relationship will continue to deepen as long as the two of you become more and more transparent with one another. Eventually, you may want to do something together, e.g., marry and start a family, or work together on a common project. Moreover, such a relationship will have its ups and downs; at times you will feel very close; at other times you will feel estranged; continued development of the relationship will require that you learn how to trust one another with your "negative" feelings about one another as well as with the "positive" feelings.

Now let's apply the analogy to our relationship with God. I will assume, on the basis of scripture and theology, that God is always interested in you and in me and in everyone in creation. You may not yet believe that; later we will talk about ways to approach God if you do not believe that God has your good at heart and is really interested in you. For now, I want to assume not only that God takes a personal and caring interest in each one of us, but also that God always pays attention to each one of us and wants to be in an intimate relationship with each of us. In other words, God is always in conscious relationship with each of us. If these assumptions are true, then each of us faces, at every moment of our existence, the question of whether we will respond to God's invitation to an intimate relationship. Perhaps it might be better to say that we face the question of whether we experience God's invitation, of whether we experience a desire for intimacy with God. If God creates each of us for an intimate relationship, then our hearts must at times burn with the desire to fulfill God's intention. Once again, the fact that you have this book in your hands indicates that you have experienced such a desire and have at least a faint interest in getting to know God better. That desire, no matter how faint, is the necessary first step toward a deepening relationship of intimacy with God. Now you must take time with God. The use of this time is what this book is all about. If you want to develop a more intimate relationship with God, then you want to embark on a process of mutual self-revelation with God, a process of growing transparency. You are embarking on a process of becoming more conscious of God's presence in your life. In other words, you will be developing your prayer life.

Let me illustrate from scripture such a growing sense of

mutual self-revelation by using the Abraham cycle in the book of Genesis. The story begins in chapter 12 where we read:

> Now the Lord said to Abram, "Go from your country and your kindred and your father's house to the land that I will show you. I will make of you a great nation, and I will bless you, and make your name great, so that you will be a blessing. I will bless those who bless you, and the one who curses you I will curse; and in you all the families of the earth shall be blessed" (12: 1–3).

Without hesitation or question Abram went. In chapter 15 Abram is depicted as being more willing to ask questions about God's promises. He reminds God that he is childless by Sarai. "You have given me no offspring, and so a slave born in my house is to be my heir." But God responds that he will have a son and that from this son will spring a people as vast as the stars. (15:1–6) Moreover, he has the courage to ask God for a sign that he will possess the land God has promised, and God gives him the sign. (15: 7–21) In chapter 16 Sarai, aware that she is barren, gives Abram her maid Hagar to sleep with and have a son. Ishmael is the result.

In chapter 17 the Lord repeats the promises, and God, as a sign of greater intimacy between them, changes Abram's name to Abraham and Sarai's to Sarah. Then comes a remarkable section which shows how familiar Abraham has become with God.

> God said to Abraham, "As for Sarah your wife, ... I will bless her, and moreover I will give you a son by her..."
> Then Abraham fell on his face and laughed, and said to himself, "Can a child be born to a man who is a hundred years old? Can Sarah, who is ninety years old, bear a

child?" And Abraham said to God, "O that Ishmael might live in your sight!"

Notice what has happened here. Abraham is able to laugh at a seemingly impossible promise of God and, in effect, to ask God to get serious. Knowing the impossibility of Sarah conceiving a child, he asks God to bless the only son he has who can be the fulfillment of God's promises, Ishmael. What is God's response? Not anger, at all. Rather, God seems to get into the spirit of the repartee. "No, but your wife Sarah shall bear you a son, and you shall name him Isaac....As for Ishmael, I have heard you; I will bless him and make him fruitful and exceedingly numerous;... But my covenant I will establish with Isaac, whom Sarah shall bear to you at this season next year" (17: 15–22). In the next chapter the promise is repeated and Sarah hears it. She too bursts into laughter. "The Lord said to Abraham, 'Why did Sarah laugh?...' But Sarah denied, saying, 'I did not laugh'; for she was afraid. He said, "Oh yes, you did laugh" (18:12–15). It is not hard to imagine God saying this with a smile. God seems to be enjoying this relationship very much.

Immediately after this scene the Lord sets out to destroy Sodom. But God says: "Shall I hide from Abraham what I am about to do, seeing that Abraham shall become a great and mighty nation...? No, for I have chosen him...."Now God desires to be fully transparent with Abraham. God tells Abraham of the intent to destroy Sodom and Gomorrah. At this point Abraham begins to haggle with God to prevent the destruction of Sodom. He even dares to tell God how God should act.

Will you indeed sweep away the righteous with the wicked? Suppose there are fifty righteous within the city; will you then sweep away the place and not forgive it for the fifty righteous who are in it? Far be it from you to do such a thing, to slay the righteous with the wicked, so that the righteous fare as the wicked! Far be that from you! Shall not the Judge of all the earth do what is just?

Can you imagine the daring and the trust Abraham had in his relationship with God to be able to speak so openly. How does God respond? By agreeing to spare the city if there are fifty righteous people there. Then Abraham keeps cutting down the number until finally God agrees to spare the city if ten righteous people are found. Notice, too, that God gave Abraham the opportunity to make this confrontation by revealing to Abraham what God intended. God has become more transparent with Abraham just as Abraham has become more transparent before God (18:16–33).

In this example we see how the relationship between God and Abraham develops through mutual self-revelation. Such self-revelation requires growing trust on Abraham's part. So, too, with us as we try to develop our relationship with God. Such trust does not spring full-blown from the first desire to get to know God better. In fact, the premise of this book is that the development of a relationship with God is a step-by-step process, with each step fueled by desire. I have tried to have each chapter address a particular desire for God's self-revelation, and see the progression of desires as the royal road toward deeper intimacy with God. Let me explain.

In the human analogy relationships grow more intimate as each of the two people allows the other to know more and more of their desire for intimacy. At first, I only let you know that I am interested in talking with you and finding out something about you. Only as I come to know more about you (and you about me) do I let you know that I want to know how you feel about me, what you value, what you love. As trust grows, I will let you know that I want you to continue to love me even though you now know that I have had unkind thoughts about you, have injured you, have angered you. I'm sure that you can continue to develop the analogy on your own. Now let's turn to the relationship with God. If our assumptions about why God created us are correct, then the deepest desire of every human heart is for complete union with God, a union which includes union with all of God's family and harmony with the universe. But we are not fully aware of the depth of that desire. Moreover, our heart's deepest desire is clouded by fears, fears that I am worthless, that God could not really want union with the likes of me, that God will make demands of me, etc. Developing our relationship with God means letting God root out these fears one by one so that finally the deepest desire of our heart can become conscious to ourselves and then be made known to God.

In each chapter of this book I will presume that a particular desire is present. If that desire fits you, then you can try out some of the prayer exercises I offer with the hope that God will fulfill that desire. I urge you not to push beyond your real desires. Take the time necessary for each desire to be fulfilled. Any relationship that aims at intimacy requires time and patience. If at first you don't get what you want, keep asking. Trust that God who has begun this good work in you will bring it to completion.

You can make the "retreat" suggested in this book any time you want. You can do it by setting aside a specific time for prayer each day or each week for a certain number of weeks. You can do it by going off to a retreat house for a weekend or for a week. Developing a relationship is a lifetime occupation, or rather an eternal one. God is always the Mystery who intrigues and draws us into deeper depths but who will never be fathomed. So in a real sense this book could last a lifetime. The desires that indicate the progression of the relationship are never fully satisfied; hence we can come back often to the same desires. Also, there are no magic times for prayer. Relationships develop through a couple of minutes of intense occupation with the other person as well as from long vacations spent together. Thus you can set aside whatever time you have available for a prayer period. It would be good to be able to schedule a half hour or more at some times just to give God more of a chance to respond to your desires. I have found also that regularity is helpful to developing the relationship with God; i.e., taking the same time each day for prayer, for example.

Ignatius of Loyola suggests a preparatory prayer before each period of prayer. His is to ask "that all my intentions, actions, and operations may be ordered purely to the service and praise of the Divine Majesty." Frederick Buechner tells of a friend of his who begins her prayer periods in this fashion. "She sits in silence for awhile, trying, without trying too hard, to be silent inside and empty and open, and then, she says, she prays: 'I sign myself with the sign of the cross,' which she does then with her hand, a large cross from forehead to navel and from shoulder to shoulder;... Then she says, 'In the name of Jesus Christ,'" and asks that something happen. (*The Alphabet of Grace*, 77). You might want to try something like this before each period of prayer and then ask for what you want. Ignatius also suggests that the person end each period of prayer with the Our Father.

Finally, after you have finished a period of prayer, it is very helpful to take a few minutes to reflect on that period of prayer and even to make some notes for your own benefit. Did you get what you desired? Note high points and low points, i.e., times when you felt energized and whole and times when you were distracted and out of sorts.

Perhaps there is some meaning in these ups and downs. They can indicate moments of grace and moments of resistance. Of course, the low points can just be due to the kind of day it is and not have great significance. If you have someone with whom you can talk about your experiences in prayer, the notes you take in these periods of reflection will come in handy as you try to discern with that person's help how God is leading you.

This brings us to question of the need for the help of others as you use this book. As you work your way through this book, you will experience many different movements in your heart and mind. Some of your experiences may surprise you, some may delight you, some may scare you. You will experience times when you are attracted to prayer and times when you are bored or even revolted at the thought of prayer. In Appendix B I have given some rules of thumb for deciding whether different interior movements are from God or not. It is often helpful to be able to talk over one's experiences in prayer with someone else in order to have a more objective insight into what is happening. This can be done in two ways, at least. The first is to have a spiritual director, someone whom you see regularly and to whom you tell what is happening in your times of prayer. Such a person can help you to sort out what is happening and to put you on the right track when you go astray. If you do seek out a spiritual director, ask around among people you trust as to who might be helpful. If you do agree to see someone, make sure that the beginning is a trial period for both of you to see if the chemistry between you will work. Also, get someone whose feet seem to be on the ground, someone with some experience of life and of prayer. Of course, if you find a good spiritual director, you might not need this book at all since the spiritual director can suggest exercises for prayer to attain what you desire.

People also get help in sharing with a group of peers their experiences of prayer. For example, you might find a group of friends who would like to move together through this book. You would gather periodically to share with one another what has happened during the period since you last got together. Such sharing of experiences of God forms a strong Christian community and can be very helpful to the journey. The one thing each of you will have to keep in mind is that we each travel the journey toward God at our own pace. We should not make comparisons about our paces. The members of the group do not make judgments about one another's prayer, but ask questions that help the one describing his prayer to clarify what he experienced. The questions can also help the person to look at the meaning of particular experiences for his relationship with God.

Now, I believe, you are ready to begin your "retreat." Find the chapter title that seems to fit best your present desire and move on from there. The first two chapters refer to desires a person might have who has some negative experiences to overcome before he or she can trust God. After that I follow the structure of the *Spiritual Exercises* of St. Ignatius. The chapters build on one another in the sense that each chapter presumes that you have received from God, at least to a certain degree, the grace you asked for in the previous chapters. As you will see, I urge you not to move beyond the desire you presently have if that desire has not been fulfilled to some extent. May God be with you.

2

"I'M NOT SURE THAT GOD CARES ABOUT ME, BUT I WISH IT WERE TRUE"

Many people find themselves in a quandary when they think about having a personal relationship with God. On the one hand, they feel some desire for such a relationship. On the other hand, they cannot believe that it is possible. Some people have a poor self-image that asserts itself whenever they think or hear of the possibility of a close relationship with God. "That's for holy people, good people, not for the likes of me." If for any reason, you have doubts about God's real desire to get close to you, while at the same time almost hoping against hope that it might be possible, this chapter may help you to approach God for help.

Begin with the preparatory prayer suggested in chapter 1. Now let's try to get at the heart of what you desire of God right now. Would you like to know that God is really personally interested in you? That God cares about you? This desire may be frail and tentative, but if you can feel its presence, then what you want from God is some sign that God does care for you. You desire a self-revelation of God. As you begin your period of prayer, tell God that this is what you want. Ignatius of Loyola, in his little handbook the *Spiritual Exercises*, suggests that before each period of prayer the person ask for what he or she wants or desires of God during this period of time. So tell God what you want now.

Perhaps you might be helped to let God know what you want by praying Psalm 13:1-3.

How long, O Lord? Will you forget me forever?
How long will you hide your face from me?
How long must I bear pain in my soul, and have sorrow in
    my heart all day long?
How long shall my enemy be exalted over me?
Consider and answer me, O Lord my God!
Give light to my eyes, or I will sleep the sleep of death.

Take some time with this prayer uttered long ago by the Hebrew psalmist. Does it come close to saying what is in your heart? Maybe the psalmist's words will suggest to you your own words. Don't be afraid to say what is in your heart.

In the first book of Samuel we read of the woman Hannah, one of Elkanah's two wives. Hannah was barren while the other wife bore many children. Hannah was deeply troubled and depressed. She must have felt that God had abandoned her. Still she "rose and presented herself before the Lord....She was deeply distressed and wept bitterly." She begged God to give her a son. She kept pouring out her heart to God. Eli, the chief priest, observed her but thought that she was drunk. "How long will you make a drunken spectacle of yourself? Put away your wine." Hannah replied: "No, my lord, I am a woman deeply troubled; I have drunk neither wine nor strong drink, but I have been pouring out my soul before the Lord. Do not regard your servant as a worthless woman, for I have been speaking out of my great anxiety and vexation all this time." Eli then bade her to go in peace. This seems to have been the sign she needed for we read: "Then the woman went to her quarters, ate and drank with her husband, and her countenance was sad no longer" (1 Sam 1:1–18). Perhaps you can take a leaf from Hannah and continue to pour out to God your own desire for some sign of God's care for you.

But take some time to be quiet as well. You need to give God a chance to answer. Perhaps you will recall some past time when God seemed very present and kind to you. Perhaps some word or thought will occur to you that will bring you peace and a sense of being in God's presence. If you happen to be in a place where you can look out on some lovely scenery, take it in; perhaps something may strike you and bring a smile of joy or happiness. Be patient. Trust in God, or at least ask God to help you to trust.

In Psalm 139 we read a section that may speak to your heart and help God to convince you of God's personal care for you:

> For it was you who formed my inward parts;
> you knit me together in my mother's womb.
> I praise you, for I am fearfully and wonderfully made
> (Ps 139:13–14).

God desired you into existence. Hence, God made you desirable, desired by God.

In the midst of their exile in Babylon the prophet called Second Isaiah was sent to give comfort to God's people. You can ask to hear the following words as directed personally to you.

> But now thus says the Lord, he who created you, O Jacob,
> he who formed you, O Israel:
> Do not fear, for I have redeemed you;

I have called you by name, you are mine.

When you pass through the waters, I will be with you; and through the rivers, they shall not overwhelm you; when you walk through fire you shall not be burned, and the flame shall not consume you.

For I am the Lord your God, the Holy One of Israel, your Savior.

I give Egypt as your ransom, Ethiopia and Seba in exchange for you.

Because you are precious in my sight, and honored, and I love you,

I give people in return for you, nations in exchange for your life.

Do not fear, for I am with you (Is 43:1-5).

You want to hear these words as personal words of God to you. Beg God to let that happen in some way that you can trust and believe.

You can try these various exercises any number of times until you are satisfied that your desire has been fulfilled, at least enough to let you believe that God is interested in a personal relationship with you. End each period of prayer with an Our Father, if you can and want to, and remember to take a short period to reflect on the prayer period just ended. Did you get what you wanted? What moved you most in a positive way? Did anything jar you or trouble you? Make notes of anything that seems significant to you. At the beginning of your next period of prayer you might be helped by looking quickly at the notes made after the last period. In this way there is more chance of having continuity in your developing relationship with God.

"I'M VERY ANGRY, MAYBE AT GOD, AND WISH I WERE NOT"

Many people have been so hurt by life that they harbor an inner anger and rage that makes it difficult for them to get close to anyone or for anyone to get close to them. I am thinking of people who have lost a beloved parent early in life, people who have been physically or psychologically abused as children, people who have suffered great physical illness as children or teenagers, people who feel that life has passed them by without giving them any kind of break, and so forth. They may not even know that they are angry and resentful at what life and the Author of life have done to them. But such people would have a difficult time trusting God. Moreover, though they are angry with God, they might not be able or willing to admit it, especially directly to God. However, until the anger and resentment are overcome to some extent, they cannot have what everyone wants, namely union with God and some peace in life. Perhaps you can identify with the desire addressed in the title of this chapter. If so, then the exercises offered here may help you to let God have a chance to respond to your desire.

First, remember to begin each period of prayer with a preparatory prayer such as those described in chapter 1.

Next you will express your desire. If the title expresses your desire, you can use that. In effect, what you are saying is this: "I have an image of you as somehow not having a loving attitude toward me, and I want you to change that image so that I can believe that you care about me and have my good at heart." Let me suggest some passages from scripture and also a poem that might help you to let God know how you feel and give God a chance to respond in ways that change your heart.

The psalmist must have wondered at one time about the ways of God. In Psalm 10 you sense that he is asking God why the evil seem to prosper while those who try to be faithful to God suffer. See if this psalm helps you to speak directly to God.

Why, O Lord, do you stand far off? Why do you hide yourself in times of trouble?

In arrogance the wicked persecute the poor—let them be caught in the schemes they have devised.

For the wicked boast of the desires of their heart, those greedy for gain curse and renounce the Lord.

In the pride of their countenance the wicked say, "God will not seek it out"; all their thoughts are, "There is no God."

Their ways prosper at all times; your judgments are on high, out of their sight; as for their foes, they scoff at them.

They think in their heart, "We shall not be moved; throughout all generations we shall not meet adversity."

Their mouths are filled with cursing and deceit and oppression; under their tongues are mischief and iniquity.

They sit in ambush in the villages; in hiding places they murder the innocent.

They stoop, they crouch, and the helpless fall by their might.

They think in their heart, "God has forgotten. he has hid-
den his face, he will never see it."
Rise up, O Lord; O God, lift up your hand;
do not forget the oppressed.
Why do the wicked renounce God, and say in their hearts,
"You will not call us to account"?   (Ps 10:1–13)

This psalm reminds me of a sonnet by the Jesuit Gerard
Manley Hopkins, who himself had some very dark days
when he wondered about God's goodness. The sonnet
begins as a translation of the complaint of Jeremiah to
God. It may help you to pray openly to God.

Thou art indeed just, Lord, if I contend
With thee; but, sir, so what I plead is just.
Why do sinners' ways prosper? and why must
Disappointment all I endeavour end?
Wert thou my enemy, O thou my friend,
How wouldst thou worse, I wonder, than thou dost
Defeat, thwart me? Oh, the sots and thralls of lust
Do in spare hours more thrive than I that spend,
Sir, life upon thy cause. See, banks and brakes
Now, leavèd how thick! lacèd they are again
With fretty chervil, look, and fresh wind shakes
Them; birds build—but not I build; no, but strain,
Time's eunuch, and not breed one work that wakes.
Mine, O thou lord of life, send my roots rain.

If these two prayers help you to pray to God, you can use
them more than once. Remember to be quiet at times to
pay attention to possible communications by God. At the
end of each prayer period say an Our Father, if you can
and want to, and take some time for reflection on the
prayer period and to make some notes for yourself.
    The book of Job treats in story form the question of the
suffering of the innocent. Its author could not accept the

prevailing wisdom that suffering came upon people because they had sinned. Job is depicted as a righteous, innocent man. In a scene that seems to make God into a person who trifles with someone's life on a dare by Satan, God allows Satan to bring a host of terrible calamities on Job to test Job's adherence to God. The book consists of dialogues between Job and his friends. His friends use all the standard arguments to prove that Job must have deserved what happened to him. Job protests his innocence over and over again. He also makes some powerful prayers to God. Perhaps some of them may help you to pray to God and to ask God to fulfill your desire. In chapter 3 we read:

> After this Job opened his mouth and cursed the day of his
> birth. Job said:
> "Let the day perish in which I was born, and the night that
> said, 'A man-child is conceived.'
> Let that day be darkness! May God above not seek it, or
> light shine on it.
> . . . .
> "Why did I not die at birth, come forth from the womb
> and expire?
> . . . .
> Why is light given to one in misery, and life to the bitter in
> soul, who long for death, but it does not come, and dig
> for it more than for hidden treasures; who rejoice
> exceedingly, and are glad when they find the grave?
> . . . .
> Truly the thing that I fear comes upon me, and what I
> dread befalls me.
> I am not at ease, nor am I quiet; I have no rest; but trouble
> comes" (Job 3:1–26).

Job does not hold back what he feels, black though it is. Later he says about God: "For the arrows of the Almighty are in me; my spirit drinks their poison; the terrors of God are arrayed against me" (6: 4).

Again he says to his so-called friends: "But I would speak to the Almighty, and I desire to argue my case with God" (13: 3). And in chapter 23 we read this bitter complaint and demand:

> Today also my complaint is bitter; his hand is heavy despite my groaning.
> Oh, that I knew where I might find him, that I might come even to his dwelling!
> I would lay my case before him, and fill my mouth with arguments.
> I would learn what he would answer me, and understand what he would say to me.
> Would he contend with me in the greatness of his power? No; but he would give heed to me.
> There an upright person could reason with him, and I should be acquitted forever by my judge.
> If I go forward, he is not there; or backward, I cannot perceive him... (23: 2–8).

Obviously Job wants God to speak to him, to show him that God still loves and cares for him in spite of the calamities that have occurred in his life. Perhaps these words can help you to speak to God openly and honestly of your pain.

Jeremiah was a reluctant prophet, as you probably know. When he first heard the call, he protested: "Ah, Lord God! Truly I do not know how to speak, for I am only a boy" (Jer 1: 6). But God persisted in calling him. For telling the truth to the leaders of the Israelites he had to suffer much. At times he must have felt abandoned by everyone, including God. At one point he utters this prayer that might give you some food for your own talk with God.

O Lord, you know; remember me and visit me,
    and bring down retribution for me on my persecutors.
In your forbearance do not take me away; know that on
    your account I suffer insult.
Your words were found, and I ate them, and your words
    became to me a joy and the delight of my heart; for I am
    called by your name, O Lord, God of hosts.
I did not sit in the company of merrymakers, nor did I
    rejoice; under the weight of your hand I sat alone,
    for you had filled me with indignation.
Why is my pain unceasing, my wound incurable, refusing
    to be healed?
Truly, you are to me like a deceitful brook, like waters that
    fail (Jer 15:15–18).

Jeremiah, obviously, had no hesitation in telling God exactly what he felt. I hope that his example will help you to speak directly to God to ask for what you want.

Remember to end each period of prayer with an Our Father (if you can honestly pray that prayer) and then take the usual time for reflection on the prayer period and for notetaking.

"I WANT . . . I KNOW NOT WHAT . . . UNION WITH THE ALL"

Sometimes we are overcome with a desire that seems to come from the depths of our being, a desire whose object we find hard to pinpoint, a desire that cannot be satisfied by anything created that we know. Sebastian Moore calls this "the desire for I know not what." We feel a great desire that seems unslakeable, yet which leaves us with a feeling of great well-being. C. S. Lewis speaks of this desire as "Joy," a desire he was surprised by when it came upon him and which finally led him to acknowledge that the object of "Joy" was God. He describes this desire as sweeter than the fulfillment of any other desire. Sebastian Moore believes that the experience of this desire for "I know not what" is an experience of God's creative desire which desires each one of us into existence. He goes on to say: "God could be defined—or rather pointed to—by this experience, as that which causes in us that desire for we know not what, which is the foundational religious experience" (*Let This Mind Be in You*, 36). Have you had such experiences? Would you want to remember such experiences or even to reexperience that desire? Perhaps the exercises in this chapter will help you.

Begin with the preparatory prayer suggested in chapter 1

and then remember to tell God what you want in this prayer period. Express the desire in any way that appeals to you. Here are some examples. "I want to feel again that deep desire for you that flooded my heart last Easter morning." "I want to experience you as the deepest desire of my heart." "I want to experience your desire that creates me and keeps me in being." These are just some examples to prod your own reflection on your desires at this moment.

One approach to let God fulfill your desire is to read slowly, even out loud, if that is possible, the first chapter of Genesis, the biblical story of creation. There we hear repeated over and over, "And God saw that it was good." Finally the peak of the story is reached:

> Then God said, "Let us make humankind in our image, according to our likeness; and let them have dominion over the fish of the sea, and over the birds of the air, and over the cattle, and over all the wild animals of the earth, and over every creeping thing that creeps upon the earth."
> So God created humankind in his image, in the image of God he created them; male and female he created them. God blessed them, and God said to them, "Be fruitful and multiply, and fill the earth and subdue it; and have dominion over the fish of the sea and over the birds of the air and over every living thing that moves upon the earth." God said, "See, I have given you every plant yielding seed that is upon the face of all the earth, and every tree with seed in its fruit; you shall have them for food. And to every beast of the earth, and to every bird of the air, and to everything that has the breath of life, I have given every green plant for food."
> And it was so. God saw everything that he had made, and indeed, it was very good (Gen 1:26–31).

Let these words stir your heart. Ask to experience God's immense desire which sets in motion the whole of creation and then sets you into this vast panorama. Perhaps you begin to feel the welling up of the desire for "I know not what," for the "All," for the Mystery we call God.

In an earlier chapter we used part of Psalm 139 as an exercise. To give God a chance to respond to your present desire to experience (again?) the deepest desire of your heart, the desire for God, you could take up the first eighteen verses of this psalm. Here the psalmist seems to be expressing an experience of God's immense desire for him.

> O Lord, you have searched me and known me.
> You know when I sit down and when I rise up; you discern my thoughts from far away.
> You search out my path and my lying down, and are acquainted with all my ways.
> Even before a word is on my tongue, O Lord, you know it completely.
> You hem me in, behind and before, and lay your hand upon me.
> Such knowledge is too wonderful for me; it is so high that I cannot attain it.

> Where can I go from your spirit? Or where can I flee from your presence?
> If I ascend to heaven, you are there; if I make my bed in Sheol, you are there.
> If I take the wings of the morning and settle at the farthest limits of the sea, even there your hand shall lead me, and your right hand shall hold me fast.
> If I say, "Surely the darkness shall cover me, and the light around me become night," even the darkness is not dark to you; the night is as bright as the day, for darkness is as light to you.

> For it was you who formed my inward parts; you knit me together in my mother's womb.

> I praise you, for I am fearfully and wonderfully made.
>   Wonderful are your works; that I know very well.
> My frame was not hidden from you, when I was being
>   made in secret, intricately woven in the depths of the
>   earth.
> Your eyes beheld my unformed substance. In your book
>   were written all the days that were formed for me, when
>   none of them as yet existed.
> How weighty to me are your thoughts, O God! How vast is
>   the sum of them!
> I try to count them—they are more than the sand; I come
> to the end—I am still with you (Ps 139:1–18).

Read the psalm slowly and let its rhythms and images play in your mind and heart. Perhaps you will feel the immense desire of God to bring you into existence, to know you personally, to draw you into harmony with God's intention for the whole human race and for you in particular.

This psalm reminds me of Francis Thompson's poem "The Hound of Heaven," in which Thompson likens God to a hound who has been seeking him out throughout his life while he tries to escape.

> I fled Him, down the nights and down the days;
> I fled Him, down the arches of the years; I fled Him, down
>   the labyrinthine ways
> Of my own mind; and in the mist of tears I hid from Him,
>   and under running laughter.
> Up vistaed hopes, I sped;
> And shot, precipitated, Adown Titanic glooms of chasmed
>   fears,
> From those strong Feet that followed, followed after. But
>   with unhurrying chase, And unperturbèd pace,
> Deliberate speed, majestic instancy, They beat—and a Voice
>   beat More instant than the Feet—
> "All things betray thee, who betrayest Me."
> At the end of the poem he hears God say:

"Ah, fondest, blindest, weakest, I am He whom thou
   seekest!
Thou dravest love from thee, who dravest Me."

Finally the poet realizes that he has wanted union with
God even as he has run away from God and that God has
been following him all along.

When we have experiences of God creating us out of
love and great desire, we spontaneously desire God and
what God wants. We want "we know not what." God's
desire for us creates in us a desire for God and for what
God wants for us. In these moments when our desires
mesh with the desire of God for us we have a sense of
immense well-being, of wholeness, of oneness with the universe. From such experiences Ignatius distilled what he
called the Principle and Foundation and which he put at
the beginning of the process of the Spiritual Exercises.
Here it is.

Human beings are created to praise, reverence, and serve
God our Lord, and by means of doing this to save their
souls.

The other things on the face of the earth are created for
the human beings, to help them in the pursuit of the end
for which they are created.

From this it follows that we ought to use these things to
the extent that they help us toward our end, and free ourselves from them to the extent that they hinder us from it.

To attain this it is necessary to make ourselves indifferent to all created things, in regard to everything which is
left to our free will and is not forbidden.

Consequently, on our own part we ought not to seek
health rather than sickness, wealth rather than poverty,
honor rather than dishonor, a long life rather than a short
one, and so on in all other matters.

Rather, we ought to desire and choose only that which is

more conducive to the end for which we are created (the *Spiritual Exercises*, n. 23).

Can you see how this might follow from reflection on your own experiences of desiring "you know not what"? When you are experiencing this desire, would you not want to do everything to attain the object of that desire, union with the Mystery at the heart of the universe? Would you not want to use everything else in your world and your gifts in conformity with God's desire for you and for the universe? Being indifferent, for Ignatius, does not mean not caring for things and people; rather it means that I put nothing in place of the object of the desire for "I know not what," and that I do not want anyone or anything else to get in the way of union with "I know not what." Ponder this text and see whether it expresses some of your own hopes for the relationship with God and with the universe God creates for you and all people.

Once again, I remind you to talk to God about your thoughts and reactions and desires. Also remember to be quiet at times to give God a chance to respond to you. At the end of the prayer period say an Our Father and then spend some moments reflecting on what happened during this prayer period. You can repeat these exercises many times until you are satisfied that you have received what you wanted. You can also follow up these exercises with those of the next chapter.

5

"HOW AND WHERE HAS GOD BEEN IN MY LIFE?"

We have twice used parts of Psalm 139 for our exercises of prayer. There the psalmist speaks of God as having had a providential hand in his life, no matter what his circumstances. Have you ever wanted to know how and where God has been in your life up to now? After all, you are the product of all the happenings, good and not so good, that have occurred in your life. Indeed, you are also the product of events that happened even before you were born. What happened to your grandparents, for example, had an effect on you through your parents and even through the culture in which you grew up. So perhaps you want to know how God has been a part of your development to this point; if so, you want to know your own salvation history. If you do have this desire, then perhaps the exercises in this chapter will help you to give God a chance to respond to your desire.

After your preparatory prayer setting the mood of prayer (cf. chapter 1) you ask God for what you want, namely to know in a felt way how God has led you through life to this present point. You might want to read again Psalm 139 to get into the mood. Another text, or series of texts that could help set the mood comes from the Joseph cycle in the book of Genesis (chapters 37 to 50). Recall that Joseph was envied by his other brothers, the sons of Jacob (Israel).

They determined to kill him, but then were persuaded to sell him as a slave to a group of wandering Ishmaelites who took him off to Egypt. In Egypt Joseph became the trusted right hand man of the Pharaoh. With wise forethought he ordered the people to store grain against a possible famine. When the famine did come, the Israelites, Joseph's brothers, had to come to Egypt to buy grain. In the course of the long and moving saga Joseph is reunited with his father and his brothers. In one scene, after Joseph has movingly revealed himself to the brothers who tried to kill him, he says:

> I am your brother, Joseph, whom you sold into Egypt. And now do not be distressed, or angry with yourselves, because you sold me here; for God sent me before you to preserve life. For the famine has been in the land these two years; and there will be neither plowing nor harvest. God sent me before you to preserve for you a remnant on earth, and to keep alive for you many survivors. So it was not you who sent me here, but God; he has made me a father to Pharaoh, and lord of all his house and ruler over all the land of Egypt (45:4–8).

Here we see a bad, even evil event for Joseph described as still being part of God's providential plan for the salvation of Israel. The further interesting aspect of this story is that all of Israel now comes down to Egypt, which sets the stage for their exploitation by the Egyptians and their redemption through Moses as told in the next book of the Bible, Exodus.

With this background I would invite you to ask God to reveal to you how God has been in your life. Then recall a place or a person from your childhood. Now, almost in the manner of free association, let the memories and images come easily to your mind and imagination. Do not try to force any particular theme. Trust that the Holy Spirit of

God who dwells in your heart will guide your thoughts and memories in order to give you what you desire. Relax and enjoy the past. If painful memories rise, ask God to enlighten you as to how God was with you even in these hard times. Of course, throughout the process you can tell God whatever occurs to you. At times you may be angry at what happened, even angry at God. Let God know how you feel. At times you may feel very grateful, not only to God but also to someone whom you remember. Let God know how you feel. If the person you remember is dead, you might even tell him or her how grateful you are, or you could ask God to convey your gratitude. These memories are part of your salvation history, the history of your relationship with God, even if you were not aware at the time of God's part in the history.

I would suggest that you not rush through your life, but take it slowly. God may have a great deal to reveal to you. You can spend more than one period of prayer just concentrating on your childhood. Then you may want to go on to your early school years. Gradually you can cover your whole life up to this time. Each period of prayer begins the same way: preparatory prayer, the expression of your desire, and then the recall of a person or a place during the period of your lifetime that is up for review. Remember that you are asking God to reveal how God has been in your life. Give God a chance. Not everything that occurs to you is necessarily the hand of God; ask God to give you the gift of discernment to sift the wheat from the chaff in your memories. In general those memories are from God that give you a sense of greater faith, hope and love, that lead to peace, joy, patience, the fruits of the Spirit Paul speaks of in the letter to the Galatians 5:22-23. (See Appendix B for some rules of thumb regarding discernment of the various inner movements of your heart.)

In Psalm 105 the psalmist sings the praises and thanks

to God for the salvation history of the Israelites. "O give thanks to the Lord, call on his name, make known his deeds among the peoples." This psalm might give you some ideas of how to praise and thank God for what God has revealed to you. At the end of each prayer period say the Our Father and then take a few moments to reflect on the period of prayer and take notes.

These exercises can deepen your appreciation of God's passionate desire for your life and for a personal relationship with you. They can, therefore, lead to a stronger desire in you for union with this God who has guided all your days with a providential hand.

6

"I WANT TO KNOW WHERE I HAVE GONE WRONG"

When we experience God's passionate love for us and our universe, we feel remarkably whole and well, and we desire to be one with God and with God's intention for us and for the universe. This experience is, however, fleeting. We soon recognize that our world and we ourselves are not in tune with God's intention. We feel ill at ease in the presence of God; we begin to wonder whether the experience of euphoria was an illusion, a self-deception. At this point we might be tempted to turn away from prayer, to consider ourselves unworthy of God's love and concern. At the same time, we still have the desire to deepen our relationship with God. We cannot completely forget the "Joy" of the desire for "I know not what." If you feel caught in this ambivalence, then perhaps this chapter's exercises will help you to move forward.

Once again, begin with the preparatory prayer mentioned in chapter 1. Then ask for what you desire. Here you might be helped to express your desire by another look at Psalm 139. This time we will look at the last two verses of the psalm:

> Search me, O God, and know my heart; test me and know my thoughts.

See if there is any wicked way in me, and lead me in the way everlasting (vv. 23–24).

Does that come near to expressing your desire? Do you want God to show you how you have deviated from the path God set you on? If you are like me, you might want this revelation, but only if it is accompanied with assurances that God still loves you. That part of your desire is implicit in the words of the psalmist. He could not be asking God to search him and know his heart with the assumption that such a searching will lead to estrangement from God. He has already expressed his desire and gratitude for God's love earlier in the psalm. Here is another way to express this desire: "I want you to show me how I have fallen short of your hopes and dreams for me; at the same time I want you to forgive me and assure me of your continuing love for me." In the *Spiritual Exercises* Ignatius expresses this desire: "to ask for growing and intense sorrow and tears for my sins" (n. 550). After the preparatory prayer ask God for what you want.

It is good to remind ourselves that sin is a blindness. Without the help of God we cannot discover our own sins and sinful tendencies. In order to know our own disorder, our own wayward ways, we need a revelation of God. Often enough we think that all we have to do to discover our sins is to examine ourselves. We need to realize that we are blind with regard to our own sinfulness, that we need the help of God. Hence, in these exercises we are expressing a desire that God reveal to us how God sees us, how God wants us to reform our lives. We may well be surprised by the revelation.

One exercise suggested by Ignatius has the retreatant meditate on the sin of the angels, then on the sin of Adam and Eve, and finally on the sin of someone who has ended up in hell for one mortal sin. His purpose is to have the retreatant reflect on the effects of sin in these three cases and apply these reflections to him/herself. Sin has had terrible consequences both for those who have sinned and for others. Belief in the devil, the fallen angels, is not strong in our age; we have, however, witnessed enough horrors in this century to have some reason to believe in a satanic power at work to draw people away from the path God wants. Perhaps the story of the fall of some of the angels through disobedience has a ring of truth to it. God's "good" creation has been terribly perverted by such a fall. The story of Adam and Eve in the garden of paradise in the second chapter of the book of Genesis recalls the experience of "Joy," the experience of a universe and the self being desired into being by God so that all people could live in communion with the Trinity, with one another and with the whole of creation. Obviously something terrible has shattered this idyll. Ignatius would have the retreatant reflect on the consequences of the sin of the first human beings as portrayed in the book of Genesis. So, too, my sins have consequences for myself, for the people around me, and for the environment. Finally, Ignatius assumes that there is at least one person in hell because he/she committed one mortal sin and died unrepentant. Reflect, he says, on how often I have deserved a similar punishment, but have been spared by the mercy of God. Perhaps such a meditation will help you to attain your desire. If it helps, go with it and tell God or Christ your reactions. If it does not help, then try some of the following exercises.

You could use an exercise similar to the one we suggested for getting to know your salvation history. After the preparatory prayer and the expression of your desire for God to reveal to you your wayward ways, you recall a person or place of your childhood and let the memories come. You trust that God's Spirit will have a hand in the

memories that come to reveal to you where you have wan-
dered from God's way. Again this exercise can be repeated
for the different periods of your life.

Once you have some sense of your sins and sinful tendencies you can use some of the gospel texts of healing as
helps to get in touch with the desire of God and of Jesus to
heal and forgive you. For example, take the healing of the
leper in Mark's gospel:

> A leper came to him begging him, and kneeling he said to
> him, "If you choose, you can make me clean." Moved with
> pity, Jesus stretched out his hand and touched him, and
> said to him, "I do choose. Be made clean!" Immediately
> the leprosy left him, and he was made clean (Mk 1:40–42).

See if you can put yourself in the leper's place in some
imaginary way. How does Jesus look at you? In the gospel
text Jesus reaches out and touches the leper; according to
the Law he thus makes himself unclean. Does this fact say
anything to you about Jesus' relation to you? One translation of this story has the leper say, "If you want to ..." to
which Jesus replies, "Of course, I want to."

Another text that sometimes helps people to let Jesus
reveal his forgiveness and love for them, precisely as sinners, is the story of the sinful woman in Simon the
Pharisee's house.

> One of the Pharisees asked Jesus to eat with him, and he
> went into the Pharisee's house and took his place at the
> table. And a woman in the city, who was a sinner, having
> learned that he was eating in the Pharisee's house, brought
> an alabaster jar of ointment. She stood behind him at his
> feet, weeping, and began to bathe his feet with her tears
> and to dry them with her hair. Then she continued kissing
> his feet and anointing them with the ointment. Now when
> the Pharisee who had invited him saw it, he said to himself,

"If this man were a prophet, he would have known who and what kind of woman this is who is touching him—that she is a sinner." Jesus spoke up and said to him, "Simon, I have something to say to you." "Teacher," he replied, "Speak." "A certain creditor had two debtors; one owed five hundred denarii, and the other fifty. When they could not pay, he canceled the debts for both of them. Now which of them will love him more?" Simon answered, "I suppose the one for whom he canceled the greater debt." And Jesus said to him, "You have judged rightly." Then turning toward the woman, he said to Simon, "Do you see this woman? I entered your house; you gave me no water for my feet, but she has bathed my feet with her tears and dried them with her hair. You gave me no kiss, but from the time I came in she has not stopped kissing my feet. You did not anoint my head with oil, but she has anointed my feet with ointment. Therefore, I tell you, her sins, which were many, have been forgiven; hence she has shown great love. But the one to whom little is forgiven, loves little." Then he said to her, "Your sins are forgiven." But those who were at the table with him began to say among themselves, "Who is this who even forgives sins?" And he said to the woman, "Your faith has saved you; go in peace" (Lk 7:36–50).

Again try to imagine the scene and yourself in it. What does it tell you about Jesus and about yourself? Notice that Jesus knows exactly who this woman is and what she has done. Yet he lets her touch him and anoint him and scandalizes Simon in the process. Let Jesus speak to you; speak to him.

You could also use the scene of the washing of the feet at the last supper in the gospel of John.

Now before the festival of the Passover, Jesus knew that his hour had come to depart from this world and go to the Father. Having loved his own who were in the world, he loved them to the end. The devil had already put it into the heart of Judas son of Simon Iscariot to betray him. And during supper Jesus, knowing that the Father had given all things into his hands, and that he had come from God and was going to God, got up from the table, took off his outer robe, and tied a towel around himself. Then he poured water into a basin and began to wash the disciples' feet and to wipe them with the towel that was tied around him. He came to Simon Peter, who said to him, "Lord, are you going to wash my feet?" Jesus answered, "You do not know now what I am doing, but later you will understand." Peter said to him, "You will never wash my feet." Jesus answered, "Unless I wash you, you have no share with me." Simon Peter said to him, "Lord, not my feet only but also my hands and my head!" Jesus said to him, "One who has bathed does not need to wash, except for the feet, but is entirely clean. And you are clean, though not all of you." For he knew who was to betray him; for this reason he said, "Not all of you are clean" (Jn 13: 1–11).

The gospel writer goes to great pains to set the scene and to indicate all that Jesus is aware of as he gets ready to wash the feet of his disciples. Judas Iscariot is among them, his heart ready to betray Jesus. Jesus knows that Peter will deny him and that the others will run away. Imagine yourself there as Jesus goes around the table. How do you react when Jesus comes to your feet? What do you want to say to him? How does he look at you?

Another text that might be a help to you is the scene after the resurrection when Jesus takes Peter aside and reverses the triple denial of Peter.

When they had finished breakfast, Jesus said to Simon Peter, "Simon son of John, do you love me more than these?" He said to him, "Yes, Lord; you know that I love you." Jesus said to him, "Feed my lambs." A second time he said to him, "Simon son of John, do you love me?" He said to him, "Yes, Lord; you know that I love you." Jesus said to him, "Tend my sheep." He said to him the third time, "Simon son of John, do you love me?" Peter felt hurt because he said to him the third time, "Do you love me?" And he said to him, "Lord, you know everything; you know that I love you." Jesus said to him, "Feed my sheep" (Jn 21: 15–17).

Can you put yourself in Peter's shoes imaginatively and let Jesus ask you the same questions?

Finally, you might want to approach Jesus on the cross and try to look into his eyes as he suffers there. What do you see in his eyes? How does he look at you? What do you want to say to him? What does he say to you? Ignatius suggests such a prayer in these words:

Imagine Christ our Lord suspended on the cross before you, and converse with him in a colloquy: How is it that he, although he is the Creator, has come to make himself a human being? How is it that he has passed from eternal life to death here in time, and to die in this way for my sins?

In a similar way, reflect on yourself and ask: What have I done for Christ? What am I doing for Christ? What ought I to do for Christ?

In this way, too, gazing on him in so pitiful a state as he hangs on the cross, speak out whatever comes to your mind (*Spiritual Exercises*, n. 53).

At the end of each period of prayer say an Our Father and then take a few moments to reflect on the prayer period. What were your reactions? Were there any strong positive or negative feelings aroused? Did you get what you desired? Again it would be helpful to jot down some notes for yourself.

7

"I WANT YOU TO REVEAL THE DISORDER IN MY WORLD"

Reflection on sin in these days cannot focus solely on one's own sins and sinful tendencies. We have become aware of the political, social and cultural dimensions of our lives and of how these dimensions impinge on us in ways that help us to lead a life in conformity with God's intention and in ways that hinder us. We are aware, in other words, that our world is not completely structured so that the intention of God that all people be united with the Trinity and with one another is easily achieved. Indeed, we are aware that very many of the social, political, economic and even religious institutions of our world are set up to make the achievement of God's intention seem a pipe dream. Our world is not the garden of Eden God intends. We can feel that things are out of sorts, but often feel helpless to do anything about the situation. Often enough, I believe, we feel out of sorts, not so much because of our personal sins, but because our world is out of joint; but we are not aware of the source of our malaise. Perhaps a new desire is beginning to form in us in our relationship with God.

Would you want God to reveal to you how God sees our world, to reveal the disorder of our society, our country, our church, our world? In the novel, *Blackrobe*, Brian Moore describes the almost insurmountable cultural clash as the French Jesuit priests tried to convert the American Indians in Canada in the seventeenth century. The hero of the novel, Père Laforgue, has witnessed the cultural clash, has been tortured and mutilated, and has come close to losing his faith. At the end of the novel he is baptizing Huron Indians, knowing that their baptism will mean the end of their civilization and, perhaps, of them. The novel ends with these words: "And a prayer came to him, a true prayer at last. 'Spare them. Spare them, O Lord. Do you love us?' 'Yes.'" In this prayer, I believe, Laforgue asks to know that God still loves this world so riven with sin, fear, misunderstanding and hatred. He knows that God has witnessed what he has witnessed, that God does not want the world to be this way, but that God still loves and stays with us.

Perhaps you may desire to have God reveal to you how God views your world. Let's begin with the usual preparatory prayer as in chapter 1. Then you express to God your desire. Here is an attempt to formulate such a desire. "Lord, I want to know the wayward ways of my world, of my community, my church, my nation, and I want to know how I contribute to these wayward ways. But, as before, I want to know that even with our wayward ways you still love us and empower us to change." You can express your own desire with this as a model.

Here is one way to give God a chance to reveal our wayward ways which has been found helpful by people. After expressing your desire start to look through the daily paper. Remember that you need God's revelation; you want to know God's reaction to the news in the paper. Read the paper in a contemplative way, letting the headlines and stories evoke images in you. As you react to these images, you may get some idea of how God reacts to these

events. Tell God how you react and ask God to show you
how you may be a participant in the continuation of some
of the horrible events depicted in the paper. Once someone told me that she had been overcome with a terrible
grief and shook with sobs during prayer as she recalled
some of the things she had witnessed in the slum where
she worked. She felt that the grief came from a depth she
did not know existed in her and concluded that God was
communicating God's reaction to these scenes. As you
contemplate the news events in the paper, something similar may happen to you.

Here is another possible exercise. The prophet Amos
bears a grim message of how God reacts to social injustice
and evil:

> For three transgressions of Israel, and for four, I will not
> revoke the punishment; because they sell the righteous for
> silver, and the needy for a pair of sandals—they who tram-
> ple the head of the poor into the dust of the earth, and
> push the afflicted out of the way; father and son go in to
> the same girl, so that my holy name is profaned; they lay
> themselves down beside every altar on garments taken in
> pledge; and in the house of their God they drink wine
> bought with fines they imposed.

In this text the Lord condemns the people of Israel for
social injustice. Moreover, the Lord also condemns religious practices that are unjust. Perhaps there is food for
thought for you here. Let God know how you react. Ask
God to enlighten you.

What is Jesus' reaction to social injustice and unaccept-
able religious institutions? Perhaps he will reveal his reaction as you contemplate the following scene:

> As he came near and saw the city (Jerusalem), he wept over
> it, saying, "If you, even you, had only recognized on this

day the things that make for peace! But now they are hidden from your eyes. Indeed, the days will come upon you
when your enemies will set ramparts around you and sur-
round you, and hem you in on every side. They will crush
you to the ground, you and your children within you, and
they will not leave within you one stone upon another;
because you did not recognize the time of your visitation
from God."

Then he entered the temple and began to drive out
those who were selling things there; and he said, "It is written, 'My house shall be a house of prayer'; but you have
made it a den of robbers" (Lk 19: 41–46).

Let the images touch your imagination. How does Jesus
look? How do you react to him? How would he react to
what you saw in the papers in the first exercise? What does
he want to communicate to you? What do you want to tell
him? What do you want to know from him?

The exercises of this chapter can complement those of
the previous chapter. You can talk to Jesus on the cross
about the matters you have reflected on in these exercises.
In the *Spiritual Exercises* Ignatius suggests a way of praying
that may be helpful to you as you go back over the exercises on personal and communal or social sin. He suggests
three colloquies (personal talks) as follows. (The words in
parentheses are additions of my own to include the notion
of social sin.)

The First Colloquy will be with our Lady, that she may
obtain for me from her Son and Lord grace for three
things:
    First, that I may feel an interior knowledge of my sins
(and of our social sins) and also an abhorrence of them;
    Second, that I may perceive the disorder in my actions (and
in the social institutions of my world), in order to detest

them, amend myself, and put myself in order (and do what I can to put my world in order);

Third, that I may have a knowledge of the world, in order to detest it and rid myself of all that is worldly and vain. Then I will say a Hail Mary. (This prayer can be found in Appendix A at the end of this book.)

The Second Colloquy. I will make the same requests to the Son, asking him to obtain these graces for me from the Father. Then I will say the prayer Soul of Christ. (Cf. Appendix A.)

The Third Colloquy. I will address these same requests to the Father, asking that he himself, the eternal Lord, may grant me these graces. Then I will say an Our Father (n. 63).

In the *Spiritual Exercises* Ignatius suggests such a triple colloquy at important points in the development of the relationship with the Lord. At this point retreatants have had rather profound experiences of God's loving design for the universe and for each of them and of the deviations introduced into God's design by the sins of people. He suggests the triple colloquy as a heartfelt prayer not to lose sight of these profound experiences.

You can end each period of prayer with an Our Father. Then take some moments to reflect on the period to note where you were more deeply moved in any way.

8

"WHAT DO I MOST WANT?"

Ignatius discovered that many people who experience the freeing power of Jesus' love for them, sinners though they are, then desire to know Jesus better in order to become his disciples. Perhaps this desire has risen in you. Perhaps you feel so grateful that Jesus has forgiven you and freed you from your sinful tendencies that now you want to get to know him better, to find out what makes him tick. If this is your desire, then you are embarked on the development of a deeper friendship and love for Jesus. Perhaps you are being called to more radical discipleship under the leadership of Jesus. In this chapter I want to introduce you to a consideration that may increase your desire to know Jesus and to let him know you.

Ignatius asks the retreatant to get in touch with his or her deepest desires, the kind of desires that are touched by fairy stories or advent prophecies. Because he was a reformed courtier and soldier who gloried in the stories of heroic men following a great king, he suggests contemplation of the fairy story of the perfect king and his call to action to save the world. He then notes that anyone worth his salt would want to follow such a king. In the second part of the contemplation he applies the analogy to Jesus Christ. Let me suggest some exercises that might allow you to get in touch with your deepest desires.

First, let's remember the preparatory prayer mentioned

in chapter 1. Then we ask for what we want. Perhaps you want to know the deepest desire of your heart. In other words, God has created us for a purpose. We have already looked at that. We have also seen that a spanner has been thrown into God's work by sin, both personal and social. But God's purpose, God's dream has not changed. That dream echoes in our hearts as our deepest desire. Perhaps you want to get in touch with that dream again and now see how that dream might be fulfilled. Express this desire in your own words.

The prophecies used in the liturgy for the season of Advent can help to evoke this dream. What the church does in Advent is to have us recall these prophecies and then to realize that in Jesus they are fulfilled. Let me suggest that you use a few of these prophecies for your prayer periods as you beg God to reveal to you your deepest dream, which is also God's. Think of the impact of Martin Luther King's great "I have a dream" speech at the Lincoln Memorial in September, 1963. Ask God to let these prophecies so touch your heart.

Here is one such prophecy, from chapter 2 of Isaiah:

> In days to come the mountain of the Lord's house shall be established as the highest of the mountains, and shall be raised above the hills; all the nations shall stream to it. Many peoples shall come and say, "Come, let us go up to the mountain of the Lord, to the house of the God of Jacob; that he may teach us his ways and that we may walk in his paths." For out of Zion shall go forth instruction and the word of the Lord from Jerusalem. He shall judge between the nations, and shall arbitrate for many peoples; they shall beat their swords into plowshares, and their spears into pruning hooks; nation shall not lift up sword against nation, neither shall they learn war any more. O house of Jacob, come, let us walk in the light of the Lord! (Is 2: 2-5).

As you let these words reverberate in your mind and heart, what reactions do you have? Does God seem to be telling you something? Let God know what is going on in your heart.

The prophet Jeremiah announces this word of the Lord:

The days are surely coming, says the Lord, when I will fulfill the promise I made to the house of Israel and the house of Judah. In those days and at that time I will cause a righteous Branch to spring up for David; and he shall execute justice and righteousness in the land. In those days Judah will be saved and Jerusalem will live in safety. And this is the name by which it will be called: "The Lord is our righteousness" (Jer 33: 14–16).

Here is another Advent prophecy from Isaiah:

A shoot shall come out from the stump of Jesse, and a branch shall grow out of his roots. The spirit of the Lord shall rest on him, the spirit of wisdom and understanding, the spirit of counsel and might, the spirit of knowledge and the fear of the Lord. He shall not judge by what his eyes see, or decide by what his ears hear; but with righteousness he shall judge the poor, and decide with equity for the meek of the earth; he shall strike the earth with the rod of his mouth, and with the breath of his lips he shall kill the wicked. Righteousness shall be the belt around his waist, and faithfulness the belt around his loins.

The wolf shall live with the lamb, the leopard shall lie down with the kid, the calf and the lion and the fatling together, and a little child shall lead them. The cow and the bear shall graze, their young shall lie down together; and the lion shall eat straw like the ox. The nursing child shall play over the hole of the asp, and the weaned child shall put its hand on the adder's den. They will not hurt or destroy on all my holy mountain; for the earth shall be full of the knowledge of the Lord as the waters cover the sea.

> On that day the root of Jesse shall stand as a signal to
> the peoples; the nations shall inquire of him, and his
> dwelling shall be glorious (Is 11: 1–10).

Are you noticing anything about your deepest dream? Are
you aware that these prophecies are used in Advent for a
reason? Do you begin to see that Jesus is the fulfillment of
these prophecies, or at least is the One whom God has
sent to bring about God's dream?

The final Advent prophecy I will suggest brings home
the reference to Jesus because he himself read from it in
the synagogue and then said: "Today this scripture has
been fulfilled in your hearing" (Lk 4: 16–21).

> The spirit of the Lord God is upon me, because the Lord
> has anointed me; he has sent me to bring good news to the
> oppressed, to bind up the brokenhearted, to proclaim liber-
> ty to the captives, and release to the prisoners; to proclaim
> the year of the Lord's favor, and the day of vengeance of
> our God; to comfort all who mourn.
>
> I will greatly rejoice in the Lord, my whole being shall
> exult in my God; for he has clothed me with the garments
> of salvation, he has covered me with the robe of righteous-
> ness, as a bridegroom decks himself with a garland, and as
> a bride adorns herself with her jewels. For as the earth
> brings forth its shoots, and as a garden causes what is sown
> in it to spring up, so the Lord God will cause righteousness
> and praise to spring up before all the nations (Is 61: 1-2;
> 10-11).

As you read this text, you might want to imagine Jesus
reading it in the synagogue. Would you want to follow
him? Would you want to know his program and to help
him fulfill it? Let him know how you are reacting.

When Ignatius suggests the contemplation of a perfect
earthly king, he is doing what the early Christians did.

They recalled the prophecies of the Hebrew Bible and then said: "Jesus is the one who fulfills this prophecy." God wants all of us to be brothers and sisters because Jesus is our brother. God wants all of us to be part of the family of God because Jesus is God's only Son. If we want to live out God's dream, we can do no better than to get to know Jesus in order to love him and to follow him. These prophecies are like fairy stories; they touch us at a very deep level and let us become aware of our deepest dream. J.R.R. Tolkien, the author of the great fantasy and fairy story, *The Lord of the Rings*, wrote of fairy stories:

> The consolation of fairy-stories, the joy of the happy ending...is a sudden and miraculous grace....It does not deny the existence...of sorrow and failure: the possibility of these is necessary to the joy of deliverance; it denies (in the face of much evidence, if you will) universal defeat and in so far is evangelium (good news), giving a fleeting glimpse of Joy, Joy beyond the walls of the world, poignant as grief.
>
> It is the mark of a good fairy-story, of the higher or more complete kind, that however wild its events, however fantastic or terrible the adventures, it can give to child or man that hears it, when the "turn" comes, a catch of the breath, a beat and lifting of the heart, near to (or indeed accompanied by) tears, as keen as that given by any form of literary art, and having a peculiar quality (*The Tolkien Reader*, 68–69).

Ignatius' parable of the perfect earthly king is such a fairy story. The prophecies used in the Advent season can be understood in the same way.

Ignatius takes the retreatant a step further. Having touched the retreatant's dream with the parable of the earthly king, he suggests an explicit turn to Christ and to Christ's plan. In his workbook for giving the Spiritual

Exercises Joseph Tetlow translates or paraphrases Ignatius' suggestions in this way:

> If a charismatic secular leader could demand loyalty (and many less excellent ones get unquestioning loyalty from their friends), what about Jesus Christ, whom God has made eternal King?
>
> I let my fancy roam. I imagine Jesus surrounded by seventy-two disciples. They sit on a hill. Jesus talks with them, saying something like this: "It is my will to win over the whole of humankind. No enemy can defeat me or finally interfere with my kingdom. I will draw all to myself. I will stay with my friends and we will labor and struggle, watch and pray. No one will have to go through anything that I do not myself go through. Whoever works with me and suffers with me will also share the glory of the kingdom with me. I assure you, I will see my project crowned with total success." After feeling how wonderfully attractive Jesus' invitation is, gently end the fantasy.
>
> Then consider that anyone with any sense at all will follow Jesus Christ. Consider this: some might want to walk more closely with Jesus Christ in this enterprise, though they cannot explain their desiring. If you feel inclined to do so, formally say this prayer to Jesus Christ:
>
> "Eternal Lord of all things, I feel your gaze on me. I sense that your mother stands near, watching, and that with you are all the great beings of heaven—angels and powers and martyrs and saints. Lord Jesus, I think you have put a desire in me.
>
> If you will help me, please, I would like to make my offering: I want it to be my desire, and my choice, provided that you want it, too, to live my life as you lived yours.
>
> I know that you lived as an insignificant person in a little, despised town;
>
> I know that you rarely tasted luxury and never, privilege, and that you resolutely refused to accept power.

I know that you suffered rejection by leaders, abandonment by friends, and failure.

I know. I can hardly bear the thought of it all.

But it seems a toweringly wonderful thing that you might call me to follow you and stand with you. I will labor with you to bring God's reign, if you will give me the gift to do it. Amen" (*Choosing Christ in the World*, 148–149).

Remember that you are not required to say this prayer. Do it only if you feel the desire to say it. If you only wish that you did desire to say it, ask the Lord to give you the desire. If you do say the prayer, you are only asking for the grace to labor with Jesus, not making a commitment at this time to any way of life.

This exercise can be repeated as often as you wish. At the end of each period of prayer say an Our Father and then take the usual few moments to reflect on the prayer period and make some notes.

9

"I WANT TO KNOW AND LOVE JESUS BETTER" IGNATIAN CONTEMPLATION: AN EXPLANATION

If you now have the desire to get to know Jesus better in order to love him more and to follow him more closely, then you are ready to embark on the contemplation of scenes of the gospels. Before we begin those exercises, however, it might be good to give a short explanation of how Ignatius views the contemplation of the gospels.

The word "contemplation" may be a problem in itself. It is used in a number of different senses, including the mystical sense of "infused contemplation." Here I mean something quite simple. Contemplation of the gospels means to read the gospels as imaginative literature, as literature that was written to make an impact on the hearts and minds of readers and hearers. The gospels were not written as theological treatises, but as stories, stories meant to stir the imagination and to elicit faith and hope in and love of Jesus Christ. Ignatian contemplation uses the gospels for this purpose.

How go about it? You begin with the usual preparatory

prayer of the kind mentioned in chapter 1. Then you ask for what you want. You want to know Jesus better in order to love him more and to follow him more closely. In other words, you want Jesus to reveal himself personally to you the way he revealed himself to his disciples. You do not want to know more about the gospels, although that might be quite useful, but to know Jesus. You want Jesus to reveal himself personally to you through the gospel texts, to use the medium of the gospel texts to let you know who he is, what he values, loves and hates. So you ask for what you want.

Ignatius uses the texts of the incarnation and the nativity to demonstrate the contemplative use of the gospels. Here I will do the same expanding on his instructions. First, let's look at the text of the incarnation.

In the sixth month the angel Gabriel was sent by God to a town in Galilee called Nazareth, to a virgin engaged to a man whose name was Joseph, of the house of David. The virgin's name was Mary. And he came to her and said, "Greetings, favored one! The Lord is with you." But she was much perplexed by his words and pondered what sort of greeting this might be. The angel said to her, "Do not be afraid, Mary, for you have found favor with God. And now, you will conceive in your womb and bear a son, and you will name him Jesus. He will be great, and will be called the Son of the Most High, and the Lord God will give to him the throne of his ancestor David. He will reign over the house of Jacob forever, and of his kingdom there will be no end." Mary said to the angel, "How can this be, since I am a virgin?" The angel said to her, "The Holy Spirit will come upon you, and the power of the Most High will overshadow you; therefore the child to be born will be holy; he will be called Son of God. And now, your relative Elizabeth in her old age has also conceived a son; and this is the sixth month for her who was said to be barren. For nothing will be impossible with God." Then Mary said, "Here am I, the servant of the Lord; let it be with me according to your word." Then the angel departed from her (Lk 1: 26–38).

Here's how Ignatius uses this passage imaginatively. He figures that the Holy Trinity must have had a parley to make the decision to send the angel. So he imagines the three Persons of the Trinity looking down on our world. What do they see? They see the whole expanse of the universe; they see people of all races, languages and sizes, people rich and poor, people happy and sad, people being born and dying, people at peace and at war. What is happening with all these people? They are like sheep without a shepherd; they are lost and do not know how to find the way; they are not living as God intends them to live. What does the Trinity do? Instead of destroying the world in anger, the Trinity decides to send the angel to a little backwater town in an enemy-occupied land and to ask a young teenage girl to become the mother of the Son of God, the savior of the world. Let your own imagination dwell on this picture of the Trinity looking out at the whole world and finally resting its gaze on the small home of Mary.

Then let your imagination be touched by the text of the gospel itself. What does Mary's home look like? What is she doing when the angel comes? Listen to the dialogue. Watch the action. Do you want to say anything to Mary, to the angel, to the three Persons of the Trinity? Are they communicating anything to you? You can let your imagination have its day. But recall that what you want is that Jesus reveal himself personally to you, that he treat you as a friend as he treated the apostles (Jn 15: 15). End the period of prayer with an Our Father and take the usual time for reflection and notetaking.

Let me say something here about the imagination. When I was a young Jesuit, I thought that Ignatian contemplation meant making up pictures in my head. Since I could not do it, I felt that I was a failure as a contemplator, that I was doomed to being a rather pedestrian pray-er for life. I also thought that others must be able to make movies in their imaginations, and that I was incapable of doing so. You may feel the same way. However, if you can get caught up in a movie or a novel, you have an imagination. If you wince when someone says that he caught his hand in a door, you have an imagination. If you weep when you hear a sad story, you have an imagination. Our imaginations differ, but all of us human beings have an imagination. We remember loved ones who are far away or dead and feel their presence; that's using our imagination. Some people can imagine the person's face and looks; others have a feel for the person, but do not imagine their looks; others can almost hear the person, but have no picture of them. For example, I do not have much of a pictorial imagination; I do not picture my dead mother, but I can sense her presence and hear her Irish brogue. Nor do I know what Jesus looks like, but I have a sense of what he was like and have felt him laughing with me. Ignatius seems to have had a very vivid pictorial imagination. I directed one person whose imagination was like that of a movie director. He went on a camping trip with Jesus for the good part of a retreat. I have also directed people like myself whose imaginations were much less pictorial and perhaps less creative. Both kinds of people have been able to engage in Ignatian contemplation. Each one of us must get along with the imagination we have and not mourn for the one that we wish we had or that we think would be a better one.

One further point about the use of the imagination for prayer. We use our imaginations to let the gospel text speak to us. We trust that the Lord's own Spirit will direct our imaginations so that we will receive what we want, namely, a personal revelation of Jesus. Not everything we imagine comes from the Holy Spirit, of course, but the Spirit who dwells in our hearts can also be seen as the major player in the twists and turns our imaginations take with the text. Again, discernment with a spiritual director or with our peer group will help us to winnow the wheat of the Spirit's action from the chaff of our own creation. Once again I refer you to Appendix B where you will find a few simple rules for discerning what is of God from what is not from God in your experience. The main point is to trust that the Lord will reveal himself to you through the imaginative contemplation of the gospel texts.

Let's now move on to the contemplation of the nativity scene. Begin with the usual preparatory prayer and then tell Jesus what you desire. Then read the text contemplatively.

> In those days a decree went out from Emperor Augustus that all the world should be registered. This was the first registration and was taken while Quirinius was governor of Syria. All went to their own towns to be registered. Joseph also went from the town of Nazareth in Galilee to Judea, to the city of David called Bethlehem, because he was descended from the house and family of David. He went to be registered with Mary, to whom he was engaged and who was expecting a child. While they were there, the time came for her to deliver her child. And she gave birth to her firstborn son and wrapped him in bands of cloth, and laid him in a manger, because there was no place for them in the inn (Lk 2: 1-7).

You can also read the rest of the Lukan account of that marvelous night and supplement it with the account in Matthew 1:18–2:12.

Ignatius suggests imagining the trip from Nazareth to Bethlehem. He had visited the Holy Land, but he does not describe what he saw there. He bids the retreatant imagine the road, whether it is level or winds through valleys and hills. He adds a servant girl to the menage. At the manger he suggests taking part in any helpful way as the child is born. I once directed a pediatrician who helped Mary with the delivery in his imagination. Let your imagination have free play with the text. What do you see and hear and sense? How do you react? Do you have any questions for the persons in the scene? Do they seem to want to tell you anything? Enter into the dialogue.

At the end of each period of prayer end with an Our Father and then, as usual, spend some moments reflecting on what happened during the period. You can go back over these scenes any number of times. In fact, Ignatius suggests that the retreatant repeat these two contemplations three more times. The last time he calls an application of the senses. It is a sort of résumé of all the imaginative creations of the first four contemplations, an imaginative savoring of the scenes.

10

"I WANT TO KNOW AND LOVE JESUS BETTER" PART II

From here on, except for some interludes, I will be suggesting texts of the gospels for the kind of Ignatian contemplation described in the last chapter. You will let your imagination be stirred by the gospel text with the desire that through this imaginative reading of the gospel Jesus will reveal himself to you. At present I am presuming that your desire is to know Jesus better in order to love him more. You may also be desirous of being called to closer discipleship with Jesus. You could include that desire in the expression of your desire at the beginning of each contemplation you make. Ignatius puts the desire at this stage of the journey in this way: "to ask for an interior knowledge of Our Lord, who became human for me, that I may love him more intensely and follow him more closely" (n. 104). In John's gospel, as you know, the word translated "to know" means "to know and love." You are asking Jesus to reveal himself to you in a personal way so that you may love him more intensely.

In this chapter I want to suggest something that you may never have done before, namely, to read practically the whole of a gospel in one setting. Most of the time we read the gospels piecemeal, one text at a time. That is the way our liturgies are set up, and when we use the gospel texts for prayer, we take particular passages, not a whole gospel. I will suggest the first ten chapters of Mark's gospel for two reasons. These ten chapters cover the public life of Jesus up to the fateful day of his triumphal entry into Jerusalem, what we call Palm Sunday, and can be read prayerfully in about forty-five minutes. Second, Mark's gospel can be seen as the gospel of discipleship, the gospel where Jesus spends much time revealing himself to his chosen disciples.

Begin your period of prayer with the usual preparatory prayer described in chapter 1 and then tell Jesus what you want, namely a personal revelation of himself so that you may love him more intensely and, if you do desire this, to follow him more closely. Remember to ask only for what you really desire, not for what you think you should desire. Also remember that you can desire to desire something; e.g., you may not yet desire to follow Jesus more closely, but you do desire to desire this.

Now begin to read the gospel text. Read slowly but steadily. By reading the first ten chapters of the gospel of Mark you will get a picture of the whole public life of Jesus as this gospel portrays it. After you finish the reading you might want to ask yourself questions like these. What stands out for me in this reading? What aspects of Jesus most moved me, positively or negatively? Do I like the Jesus portrayed? Dislike him? Are there some traits I like, others I dislike? Do some of his actions puzzle me? Would I want to ask him to explain himself? In the time left in the prayer period talk to the Jesus who has revealed himself to you. At the end of the prayer period end with an Our Father and then, as usual, spend a few moments reflecting on the prayer period and make some notes for yourself.

I would suggest that you return to this overall picture of Jesus the next few times that you set aside for prayer. Now you can spend more time in dialogue with the Jesus who has been revealed to you. Be as open as you can be with him. Also take time to be quiet so that Jesus can somehow touch your heart with his responses. I am not talking of hearing his actual voice in your inner ear, although some people seem to have such experiences. I mean that in these times of quiet you may recall something that you had not noticed before, much as the two disciples who walked with Jesus on the road to Emmaus recalled that their hearts were burning while on the road, something that they had not noticed until after Jesus broke the bread and then disappeared (Lk 24: 13–32). Or you may think of something new about Jesus that will be an answer to one of your questions. Or you may have the sense of Jesus smiling at you or putting his arm around your shoulder. There are many ways that the Lord can reveal himself to us. Each one of us is different, so that the way of revelation will differ for each of us. But we need to give Jesus some time to reveal himself to us by being quiet during these periods of prayer.

You want Jesus to reveal himself to you personally so that your love for him may become more intensified and that, perhaps, you may follow him more closely. In this chapter I have suggested one way to give Jesus a chance to fulfill that desire, or rather, to begin to fulfill that desire. Getting to know Jesus is the task of a lifetime and even beyond. As John says at the end of his gospel: "But there are also many other things that Jesus did; if every one of them were written down, I suppose the world itself could not contain the books that would be written" (Jn 21: 25). No one, in this life at any rate, can ever fully know another human being; there is always more to be revealed because each human being is mysterious. How much more is this true of Jesus, who is Mystery itself! You could, if you want, try this method of reading a whole gospel with one or other of the other gospels. They require a bit more time to get through in one sitting, but each of them has a somewhat different focus on this Jesus who has enthralled billions of people since his birth to Mary of Nazareth. But keep in mind that you are reading these gospels not for intellectual comparisons, but to give Jesus a chance to reveal himself personally to you.

11

"I WANT TO KNOW AND LOVE JESUS BETTER" PART III

If you followed the suggestion of the last chapter, you have an overview of the public life of Jesus as presented in Mark's gospel. Presuming that you have the desire for a personal revelation of Jesus so that you may love him more intensely and follow him more closely, I will suggest in this chapter an attention to the details of the description of Jesus' public life as presented in the first three chapters of the gospel of Mark. I suggest the use of Mark's gospel because it concentrates on the actions of Jesus during his public life and seems to focus on the call to discipleship more clearly than the other gospels.

Let me suggest a structure for your prayer periods as you use the material presented in this chapter. If you were making an Ignatian retreat full time, your director would probably give you new material for the first two periods of prayer each day and then suggest repetitions for the next two or three periods of prayer that day. So, for example, Ignatius suggests contemplation of the incarnation and of the nativity for the first two periods of a day and three repetitions for the rest of that day. I suggest that you try that structure in whatever way you are making this "retreat." So, if you are trying to pray for a half hour to an hour each day in the week, take new passages for the first two days and follow that by repeating the contemplation of those two passages for the next two or three days. If, as another example, you are praying for a half hour to an hour once a week, take new passages for the first two weeks and then follow with repetitions for the next two or three weeks. You could think of any five consecutive periods of prayer in this format as one day of a retreat at a retreat house. You can make adjustments to this structure according to your own schedule. Structure is to be of help to your developing relationship with Jesus; it should not become an end in itself. But such a structure has proved a help to many people. I suggest you try it to see if it works for you.

Begin each period of prayer with the introductory prayer suggested in chapter 1 and then express your desire. Here the desire is for a personal revelation of Jesus so that you may love him more intensely and follow him more closely.

For the first period of prayer I suggest taking Mark 1: 9–14.

In those days Jesus came from Nazareth of Galilee and was baptized by John in the Jordan. And just as he was coming up out of the water, he saw the heavens torn apart and the Spirit descending like a dove on him. And a voice came from heaven, "You are my Son, the Beloved; with you I am well pleased."

And the Spirit immediately drove him out into the wilderness. He was in the wilderness forty days, tempted by Satan; and he was with the wild beasts; and the angels waited on him.

Now after John was arrested, Jesus came to Galilee, proclaiming the good news of God, and saying, "The time is fulfilled, and the kingdom of God has come near; repent, and believe in the good news."

(An aside: recall that "good news" is the translation of the Greek "euangelion" which was translated into Latin as "evangelium" and into early English as "gospel." Thus the "good news" is the gospel, the life and action of Jesus Christ.)

Let this text spark your imagination. What was it like there in the Jordan valley as all these people came to be baptized by John? How does the baptism of Jesus strike you? How does Jesus look as he experiences the descent of the dove and the voice of his Father? What does this experience do for his sense of identity and mission? Remember that Jesus is a full human being and that our best bet for getting a sense of what these experiences meant to him is through our reactions, moved by the Holy Spirit. What was it like for Jesus in the wilderness? Do you wonder how Jesus could be tempted? Do you want to know what these temptations meant to him? Ask him to reveal himself to you. If you wish, you could look at Luke's account of the temptations in chapter 4: 1–13, where there is a longer description of them. Finally, notice that these two experiences of the baptism and the temptations in the wilderness are followed by the opening of his public life of preaching the good news. How does Jesus look to you as he makes this opening proclamation. What does he mean by the call to repentance? Do you sense the nearness of the kingdom of God?

It might help you to trust your own imagination if I mention how the Japanese novelist (and convert to Catholicism) Shusaku Endo portrayed these incidents in his imaginative *A Life of Jesus.* He pictures John the Baptizer as a man who preaches a stern and demanding God. Through his baptism and his time in the wilderness Jesus came to experience God as more kind and merciful, as his Abba (his Dad). According to Endo this was the good news that Jesus now set out to preach. Thus, according to Endo's imaginative contemplation of the gospel texts, Jesus learned through his own experience that God was not the God preached by the Pharisees, nor even the exclusively stern and wrathful God preached by John the Baptizer. That Jesus learned from experience only means that he was a human being like us. As Luke says: "And Jesus increased in wisdom and in years, and in divine and human favor" (Lk 2: 52). As you finish your period of prayer, say an Our Father and then, as usual, take some time for reflection on what happened during the prayer and to make some notes.

For the second contemplation note that the very next thing Mark's Jesus does is to call his first disciples.

> As Jesus passed along the Sea of Galilee, he saw Simon and his brother Andrew casting a net into the sea—for they were fishermen. And Jesus said to them, "Follow me and I will make you fish for people." And immediately they left their nets and followed him. As he went a little farther, he saw James son of Zebedee and his brother John, who were in the boat mending the nets. Immediately he called them; and they left their father Zebedee in the boat with the hired men, and followed him (Mk 1: 16–20).

What kind of man could have such power over people? How does Jesus seem to you? Are you attracted to him? Afraid of him? Do you want to be called by him? Let your imagination play with the scene and engage with Jesus in a dialogue. Again, at the end of the period of prayer say an Our Father and take some moments for reflection on the prayer and to make some notes.

For the two or three repetitions you begin with the usual preparatory prayer and the expression of your desire. Then you can either read the passages of the first two periods or look at your notes or do both. Spend time on those aspects

of the scenes that moved you most, whether the movements were positive or negative. Some aspects of Jesus may
have strongly attracted you, for example. Go back over
these. Some aspects may have turned you off or frightened
you. Go back to these and ask Jesus for help to understand
your reactions and him. The purpose of the repetitions is
to savor the contemplation of Jesus and to deepen the interior knowledge and love you have of Jesus. At the end of
each period of repetition say an Our Father and take the
usual time for reflection.

One way to see the structure of the next sections of
Mark's gospel is to imagine that the new disciples now
watch what Jesus is saying and doing. For your next two
periods of prayer I suggest you take the expulsion of the
demons (1: 21–28; 32–34). Begin with the usual preparatory prayer and then express your desire. The text follows:

> They went to Capernaum; and when the sabbath came, he
> entered the synagogue and taught. They were astounded at
> his teaching, for he taught them as one having authority,
> and not as the scribes. Just then there was in their syna-
> gogue a man with an unclean spirit, and he cried out,
> "What have you to do with us, Jesus of Nazareth? Have you
> come to destroy us? I know who you are, the Holy One of
> God." But Jesus rebuked him, saying, "Be silent, and come
> out of him!" And the unclean spirit, convulsing him and
> crying with a loud voice, came out of him.
>
> They were all amazed, and they kept asking one anoth-
> er, "What is this? A new teaching—with authority! He com-
> mands even the unclean spirits, and they obey him." At
> once his fame began to spread throughout the surround-
> ing region of Galilee....
>
> That evening, at sundown, they brought to him all who
> were sick or possessed with demons. And the whole city
> was gathered around the door. And he cured many who
> were sick with various diseases, and cast out many demons;

and he would not permit the demons to speak, because they knew him.

The disciples begin to see what following Jesus means as well as what kind of man he is. They see what moves him. They see his power over the evil one and over illness. Let your own imagination put you into the scene. Let Jesus know your reactions. Listen for his response. Finish the prayer period with an Our Father and then take the usual time for reflection and notetaking.

For your next period of prayer take the following scenes. Begin with the usual preparatory prayer and the expression of your desire. Then read the text contemplatively.

In the morning, while it was still very dark, he got up and went out to a deserted place, and there he prayed. And Simon and his companions hunted for him. When they found him, they said to him, "Everyone is searching for you." He answered, "Let us go on to the neighboring towns, so that I may proclaim the message there also; for that is what I came out to do." And he went throughout Galilee, proclaiming the message in their synagogues and casting out demons.

A leper came to him begging him, and kneeling he said to him, "If you choose, you can make me clean." Moved with pity, Jesus stretched out his hand and touched him, and said to him, "I do choose. Be made clean!" Immediately the leprosy left him, and he was made clean. After sternly warning him he sent him away at once, saying to him, "See that you say nothing to anyone; but go, show yourself to the priest, and offer for your cleansing what Moses command-ed, as a testimony to them." But he went out and began to proclaim it freely, and to spread the word, so that Jesus could no longer go into a town openly, but stayed out in the country; and people came to him from every quarter (1: 35–45).

The new disciples see him spend time alone in prayer. They notice how the crowds seek him out. They watch him touch a leper with great compassion, unafraid of what people will think of him and unafraid of contracting the disease himself. They see his fame spread. Let these texts touch your imagination and thus let Jesus reveal himself to you. Note your reactions to him and to these events. In this process you are growing in your interior knowledge and love of Jesus. Perhaps you are also growing in your desire to follow him more closely, to be called by him to more radical discipleship. Remember to end each period of prayer with an Our Father and with a short period of reflection. After finishing these two new scenes go back over them in repetitions for the next two or three periods of prayer. By now this pattern of two new scenes followed by two or three periods of repetition should be getting familiar.

With chapter 2 of Mark's gospel the new disciples begin to see that Jesus stirs up controversy with the religious leaders of his own religion. For your next two new texts I suggest that you divide up this chapter taking first the scene where some people let down a paralyzed man into the house (2: 1–12) and then the rest of the chapter (13–28). Begin your first period of prayer with the usual preparatory prayer and the expression of your desire. Then read the following text contemplatively.

When he returned to Capernaum after some days, it was reported that he was at home. So many gathered around that there was no longer room for them, not even in front of the door; and he was speaking the word to them. Then some people came, bringing to him a paralyzed man, carried by four of them. And when they could not bring him to Jesus because of the crowd, they removed the roof above him; and after having dug through it, they let down the mat on which the paralytic lay. When Jesus saw their faith, he said to the paralytic, "Son, your sins are forgiven." Now some of the scribes were sitting there, questioning in their hearts, "Why does this fellow speak in this way? It is blasphemy! Who can forgive sins but God alone?" At once Jesus perceived in his spirit that they were discussing these questions among themselves; and he said to them, "Why do you raise such questions in your hearts? Which is easier, to say to the paralytic, 'Your sins are forgiven,' or to say, 'Stand up and take your mat and walk'? But so that you may know that the Son of Man has authority on earth to forgive sins"—he said to the paralytic—"I say to you, stand up, take your mat and go to your home." And he stood up, and immediately took the mat and went out before all of them; so that they were all amazed and glorified God, saying, "We have never seen anything like this!" (2: 1–12).

Try to enter the scene imaginatively, to feel the emotions of the participants. How do the friends of the paralytic and the paralytic himself feel when they cannot get through the door? How does Jesus react when he sees the mat coming down through the roof? Note the reaction of the scribes and the atmosphere they bring to the room. How does Jesus feel as he finds himself at odds with the leaders of his religion? How do the new disciples react to these events? Speak to anyone in the scene and, of course, with Jesus. Give him time to respond to you. End the prayer period with an Our Father and the usual period of reflection.

For your next period of prayer begin with the usual preparatory prayer and the expression of your desire. Then read the following text contemplatively.

Jesus went out again beside the sea; the whole crowd gathered around him, and he taught them. As he was walking along, he saw Levi son of Alphaeus sitting at the tax booth, and he said to him, " Follow me." And he got up and followed him. And as he sat at dinner in Levi's house, many tax collectors and sinners were also sitting with Jesus and his disciples—for there were many who followed him. When the scribes of the Pharisees saw that he was eating with sinners and tax collectors, they said to his disciples, "Why does he eat with tax collectors and sinners?" When Jesus heard this, he said to them, "Those who are well have no need of a physician, but those who are sick; I have come to call not the righteous but sinners...."

One sabbath he was going through the grainfields; and as they made their way his disciples began to pluck heads of grain. The Pharisees said to him, "Look, why are they doing what is not lawful on the sabbath?" And he said to them, "Have you never read what David did when he and his companions were hungry and in need of food? He entered the house of God, when Abiathar was high priest, and ate the bread of the Presence, which it is not lawful for any but the priests to eat, and he gave some to his companions." Then he said to them, "The sabbath was made for humankind, and not humankind for the sabbath; so the Son of Man is lord even of the sabbath" (2: 13–17; 23–28).

Notice whom he befriends and sits at table with, and what effect his habits of table fellowship have on all the people in the scene. How do you feel about him? How do the disciples feel as they see themselves getting involved with a man who stirs up such enmity in their religious leaders? How do you feel? At the end of each period of prayer end with an Our Father and then spend some moments in reflection on and in taking notes of what happened during the period. Use these notes for your two or three repetitions.

In the structure of Mark's gospel the new disciples have seen Jesus openly challenge the power of evil as represented by the devil, heal the sick, make enemies of the religious establishment both by the kinds of people with whom he associated and by actions that ran counter to the establishment's interpretation of who God is. We now come to the climactic scene where Jesus chooses the twelve apostles, which I suggest for the first of the next two new texts. Begin with the usual preparatory prayer and the expression of your desire. Then read this text contemplatively.

> He went up the mountain and called to him those whom he wanted, and they came to him. And he appointed twelve, whom he also named apostles, to be with him, and to be sent out to proclaim the message, and to have authority to cast out demons. So he appointed the twelve: Simon (to whom he gave the name Peter), James son of Zebedee and John the brother of James (to whom he gave the name Boanerges, that is, Sons of Thunder); and Andrew, and Philip, and Bartholomew, and Matthew, and Thomas, and James son of Alphaeus, and Thaddaeus, and Simon the Cananaean, and Judas Iscariot, who betrayed him (3: 13–19).

Like the disciples you have watched Jesus in action, you have come to know him more intimately, perhaps to love him more and to desire to follow him more closely. Let this scene spark your imagination. Note the different participants. How are they reacting as the scene unfolds? Notice that Jesus picks out the twelve to do the same tasks as he alone has had up to now. He gives nicknames to Simon (Peter, which could be translated as "Rocky") and to James and John. Does this tell you anything about Jesus? How do the twelve react to being called? How do those not chosen react? Where are you in the crowd? Do you want to be called to be with Jesus, to be an apostle, to imitate Jesus in proclaiming the good news and in confronting evil directly? At the end of the prayer period say an Our Father and then do the usual reflection on what happened during the period.

For your next period of prayer I suggest that you take the rest of chapter 3 which portrays the consequences of Jesus' actions. After the usual preparatory prayer and the expression of your desire read this text contemplatively.

> Then he went home; and the crowd came together again, so that they could not even eat. When his family heard it, they went out to restrain him, for people were saying, "He has gone out of his mind." And the scribes who came down from Jerusalem said, "He has Beelzebul, and by the ruler of the demons he casts out demons." And he called them to him, and spoke to them in parables, "How can Satan cast out Satan? If a kingdom is divided against itself, that kingdom cannot stand. And if a house is divided against itself, that house will not be able to stand. And if Satan has risen up against himself and is divided, he cannot stand, but his end has come. But no one can enter a strong man's house and plunder his property without first tying up the strong man; then indeed the house can be plundered...."
>
> Then his mother and his brothers came; and standing outside, they sent to him and called him. A crowd was sitting around him; and they said to him, "Your mother and your brothers and sisters are outside, asking for you." And he replied, "Who are my mother and my brothers?" And looking at those who sat around him, he said, "Here are my mother and my brothers! Whoever does the will of God is my brother and sister and mother" (Mk 3: 19–34).

Again enter the scenes imaginatively with the desire that Jesus reveal to you who he is, what he values, how he relates to you. Notice that his family thinks that he is crazy and that the leaders of his religion think that he is possessed by a demon. How does he react to these charges? Engage in the dialogue with him. After ending the prayer with an Our Father spend some time reflecting on the prayer and making notes.

Use the notes to start you off in the two or three repetitions you make on these two scenes. Remember that the purpose of these repetitions is to help you to deepen your interior knowledge of Jesus, to learn more about him and about yourself in relation to him. Pay particular attention to any strong reactions you have. Of course, if you have no strong reactions at all, you ought to be concerned. Jesus is anything but boring. You may be resisting further closeness to Jesus. Talking with your spiritual director or with your peer group about such flatness of affect can help you to see whether you are resisting a new step in your relationship with Jesus.

12

"I WANT TO SHARE THE VALUES OF JESUS"

At this point in the development of your relationship with Jesus I would like to suggest, as Ignatius does in the *Spiritual Exercises*, that you spend the next few prayer periods reflecting on the struggle between good and evil that pervades our world and our very hearts. In Mark's gospel you have seen Jesus in a pitched battle with the demons, have seen him being tempted in the wilderness by Satan. At about this time in the progression of the Spiritual Exercises Ignatius proposes a meditation on "Two Standards, the one of Christ,...the other of Lucifer, the mortal enemy of our human nature" (n. 136). Ignatius was a former soldier. As a result he often uses military metaphors to describe the spiritual life. Here "standard" refers to the flag under which an army marches, and it stands for the values of the leader of the army. Thus, Ignatius is suggesting a meditation on the values and strategies of Christ and of Satan. The desire here "will be to ask for insight into the deceits of the evil leader, and for help to guard myself against them; and further, for insight into the genuine life which the supreme and truthful commander sets forth, and grace to imitate him" (n. 139). If you have this desire, this chapter will indicate some exercises that will give the Lord a chance to fulfill your desire.

First, begin with the usual preparatory prayer described

in chapter 1 and then express your desire. Ignatius has the retreatant imagine first how Satan sits "on a throne of fire and smoke, in aspect horrible and terrifying" (n. 140). Then "consider how he summons uncountable devils, disperses some to one city and others to another, and thus throughout the whole world, without missing any provinces, places, states, or individual persons" (n. 141). Finally, consider

> the address he makes to them: How he admonishes them to set up snares and chains; how first they should tempt people to covet riches (as he usually does, at least in most cases), so that they may more easily come to vain honor from the world, and finally to surging pride. In this way, the first step is riches, the second is honor, and the third is pride; and from these three steps the enemy entices them to all the other vices (n. 142).

In spite of the medieval and military imagery these suggestions for meditation have a power to touch our reality. While Ignatius stresses the attachment to riches and honor as leading to pride, the inordinate attachment can be directed to a person or place or thing, to one's self-image, to one's talent or looks, to one's family or nation, and even to one's self-pity or suffering. Recall Uriah Heep, Charles Dickens' creation, and his attachment to his humble origins; "I'm 'umble and my mother's 'umble too". He was a spiteful and vengeful character. To help you to reflect on the strategy here presented, I offer a couple of other stories.

Woody Allen's film *Crimes and Misdemeanors* depicts the progression Ignatius presents. At the beginning of the movie a prominent doctor and philanthropist, played by Martin Landau, is being feted at a banquet. He is seated at table with his wife and family, but while the talks praising him go on, he is thinking of the threats posed by his mistress, played by Angelica Huston. She wants him to leave his wife and marry her and has threatened to tell his wife about their affair. The doctor is in a quandary. If he were to leave his wife and family, he would lose face in the community; he might even lose money. He does not know what to do. In the movie he contacts his rather seedy brother who has mob connections and tells him his problem. The brother suggests that he could arrange the mistress' murder in such a way that no one would ever suspect the doctor. He recoils in horror at the suggestion. But as the noose tightens around him through the increasingly demanding mistress, he finally tells his brother to make the arrangements. A "hit man" from another city is hired who kills the mistress.

Reflect on this story. Note that the doctor has gained a great deal of wealth through his intelligence and dedication as well as from his wife. The wealth has enabled him to be a benefactor and thus to gain honor in the larger community, symbolized in the opening scene of the movie by the banquet honoring him. His wealth has also made it possible for him to have a mistress whom he takes on business trips. He has told the mistress that he no longer loves his wife. The mistress now wants him to act on the fact that he loves her, not his wife. Because he does not want to lose either his wealth or his reputation, he does something that his conscience at first recoils from, namely, to take the life of another person unjustly. He has come to overweening pride, to the belief that his position justifies murder. Ponder the progression of temptation here and ask yourself whether you can sense any ripples of such a progression of temptation in yourself or in your experience.

Georges Bernanos' novel, *Diary of a Country Priest* provides more than one example of the progression of temptation, but one stands out. Madame la comtesse lost her only son, the light of her life, when he was a child. Her husband is a philanderer; her daughter has fastened all her affections on her father and excluded her mother from their circle. The comtesse harbors a deep resentment and hatred for her husband and her daughter, but because of her position she has never let anyone, even her confessor, know. Outwardly, she has kept the proprieties. In the climactic scene with the country priest they have been talking about the fact that her daughter is being sent away to England by her husband because of the daughter's jealousy about the affair of her father with her governess. Here is the dialogue.

> "At least," she began to tap her foot, "I suppose we're to be judged by our actions. How have I sinned? It's true my daughter and I are strangers. But so far we haven't let anyone see it. And now in this crisis I'm obeying my husband. If he should be wrong—oh, of course he thinks his daughter will come back to him!"
>
> Something in her expression changed. She bit her lips, too late.
>
> "And do *you* think so, madame?"
>
> God! She jerked back her head, and I saw—saw in a flash—her admission rise in spite of herself from the deep of her implacable soul. Caught in the act of lying, eyes said "yes," while "no" came from between parted lips, as from the invincible depths of her.
>
> I think that she was amazed by her own "no," but she did not try to take it back. Of all hate domestic hate is the most dangerous, it assuages itself by perpetual conflict, it is like those open abscesses without fever which slowly poison.

What is at stake here is the threat that her daughter will commit suicide if she is sent away. The comtesse, harboring her own resentment at the loss of her beloved son and

of the love of her husband, is willing to let her daughter go,
even though she is sure that the daughter will never come
back and will probably commit suicide.

The country priest now goes for the neuralgic point of
her hatred, her bitter resentment at the death of her son.
He tells her that her hatred will keep her separated from
her son forever. She says:

> "Love is stronger than death—that stands written in your
> books."
>
> "But it isn't we who invented love. Love has its own
> order, its own laws."
>
> "God is love's master."
>
> "No, not its master. God is love itself....If you want to
> love don't place yourself beyond love's reach."
>
> She rested both hands on my arm, her face was almost
> touching mine: "This is absurd. You talk to me as though I
> were a criminal. So all my husband's unfaithfulness goes
> for nothing—and my daughter's coldness, her rebellion, all
> that goes for nothing, nothing, nothing."

The priest then tells her that he believes that God has let
him know the peril she is in and goes on to make this
statement.

> "Oh, madame, nobody can see in advance what one bad
> thought may have as its consequence. Evil thoughts are like
> good ones: thousands may be scattered by the wind, or
> overgrown or dried up by the sun. Only one takes root.
> The seeds of good and evil are everywhere. Our great mis-
> fortune is that human justice always intervenes too late.
> We only repress or brand the act, without ever being able
> to go back further than the culprit. But hidden sins poison
> the air which others breathe, and without such corruption
> at the source, many a wretched man, tainted unconscious-
> ly, would never have become a criminal."

Here the priest tells her that at least some of the hatred in her daughter may be due to her own hidden sin. She says:

"Would you deign to show me my hidden sin? The worm in the fruit?"

"You must resign yourself to—to God. Open your heart to Him."

I dared not speak more plainly of her dead child, and the word "resign" seemed to astonish her.

"Resign myself? To what?" Then suddenly she understood....

"Resign myself?" Her gentle voice froze. "What do you mean? Don't you think me resigned enough? If I hadn't been resigned! It makes me ashamed....I tell you I've often envied weaker women who haven't the strength to toil up these hills. But we're such a tough lot! I should have killed my wretched body, so that it shouldn't forget. Not all of us can manage to kill ourselves—"

"That's not the resignation I mean, as you well know," I said to her.

"Well then—what? I go to mass, I make my Easter. I might have given up going to church altogether—I did think of it at one time. But I considered that sort of thing beneath me."

"Madame, no blasphemy you could utter would be as bad as what you've just said! Your words have all the callousness of hell in them....How dare you treat God in such a way? You close your heart against Him and you—"

"At least I've lived in peace—and I might have died in it—"

"That's no longer possible."

She reared like a viper: "I've ceased to bother about God. When you've forced me to admit that I hate Him, will you be any better off, you idiot?"

"You no longer hate Him. Hate is indifference and contempt. Now at last you're face-to-face with Him."

The scene goes on. She faces the fact that she has never really given up her son, has tried to keep him by the force of her own will. She has not said the Our Father since the day he died because of the words, "Thy will be done." As she struggles to surrender to God, she feels that she is losing her son all over again. At the climax of the scene she says:

> "I'll either give Him all or nothing. My people are made that way."
> "Give everything."
> "Oh, you don't understand! You think you've managed to make me docile. The dregs of my pride would still be enough to send you to hell."
> "Give your pride with all the rest! Give everything!"

In a desperate gesture, which the priest is unable to stop, she flings the medallion which contains a lock of her son's hair into the fire. But she is at peace.

Perhaps this long scene will help you to meditate on the values of the evil one, the values opposite to those of Christ. Ponder the kind of possessiveness that can lead to overbearing pride that would, if it could, take her child to a place where God did not exist. Then reflect on yourself and your life.

Next Ignatius has the retreatant reflect on Christ and his values. First, consider "how Christ our Lord takes his place in that great plain near Jerusalem, in an area which is lowly, beautiful, and attractive" (n. 144). Christ's appearance is the opposite of Satan's. Then consider

> how the Lord of all the world chooses so many persons, apostles, disciples, and the like. He sends them throughout the whole world, to spread his doctrine among people of every state and condition (n. 145).

Finally consider

> the address which Christ our Lord makes to all his servants
> and friends whom he is sending on this expedition. He rec-
> ommends that they endeavor to aid all persons, by attract-
> ing them, first, to the most perfect spiritual poverty and
> also, if the Divine Majesty should be served and should
> wish to choose them for it, even to no less a degree of actu-
> al poverty; and second, by attracting them to a desire of
> reproaches and contempt, since from these results humili-
> ty.
>
> In this way there will be three steps: the first, poverty in
> opposition to riches; the second, reproaches or contempt
> in opposition to honor from the world; and the third,
> humility in opposition to pride. Then from these three
> steps they should induce people to all the other virtues (n.
> 146).

What Ignatius puts into the mouth of Jesus is the same
strategy that the country priest used with the comtesse. It
is to let nothing stand in the way of surrender to God
because what we most deeply want is union with God. But
inordinate attachment to possessions, to our reputation, to
anything that is not God will lead inexorably to pride,
which cuts us off from what we most want, namely, God.
"Perfect spiritual poverty" is the opposite of inordinate
attachment; it is also equivalent to the "indifference"
Ignatius speaks of in the Principle and Foundation. You
should note that actual poverty is not a choice that we
make on our own; it is up to God to choose us for that.
Moreover, the strategy of Christ is not to do stupid and asi-
nine things in order to be held in contempt; rather, the
strategy is to bring people to *desire* to be treated as a fool
for Christ because the inordinate desire for honor and a
good reputation can lead them away from union with God.
Here is an example of someone who experienced the

value system of Jesus. It was told to me by a young Jesuit
professor of philosophy from the United States who spent
three months working in a very poor parish, El Agustino,
in Lima, Peru.

> Most mornings of my stay in Lima, I spent visiting and car-
> ing for the sick at a local hospital, which specialized in TB
> cases from the most desperately poor segments of the city.
> One of the first patients that I encountered was a three-
> year-old girl apparently dying from meningitis, the result
> of complications from either a neglected or misdiagnosed
> case of TB. After baptizing and anointing her, I began to
> visit her daily, in part because I realized that she had been
> abandoned by her family and left to die by the medical
> staff. Feverish and suffering frequent seizures due to the
> brain infection, the child lay hour after hour alone in her
> crib....I often prayed for her death—perhaps more as an
> end to my anguish than to hers. I gradually arranged my
> schedule to spend as much time as possible at her side,
> speaking to her, cleaning her and drying her head and
> face, but often just looking at her, beholding the mystery
> and the beauty of her countenance, or at the bruised veins
> of her hands and feet where an I.V. was rotated daily from
> hand to foot, from foot to hand. And then, I don't know
> how, I was allowed a deeper vision of things: Christ cruci-
> fied, abandoned and cast out was one with the child. It was
> not that her body or sufferings had become a symbol of
> Christ's death on the cross, but that in her God's very pres-
> ence and mercy became real in a world of darkness and
> silence. I experienced in the dejection and abandonment
> of the child an objective, sensible intuition which both
> summoned and integrated me into the event which I
> beheld.
> A few days later I was in the wealthy section of Lima
> searching for medicines when I began to view the world
> around me, its riches, vanity and pride, as a meaningless
> deception, an illusion of security and well-being next to the

poverty and suffering that I had left in El Agustino. Over the next weeks, I realized that I was in fact engaged in a meditation on the Two Standards.

One final exercise might be to contemplate two scenes in Mark's gospel which bring out the opposing values. The first is the banquet of Herod (Mk 6: 17–29). Here Herod is being honored on his birthday, happy in his wealth and his high place in the world. But he finally does something that he does not want to do because he fears losing face before his guests. Salome has asked for the head of John the Baptizer. "The king was deeply grieved; yet out of regard for his oaths and for the guests, he did not want to refuse her." So he orders that John be beheaded. Immediately after this scene we see Jesus and the disciples go off to rest for a while (6: 30–44). But the people get wind of where they are and follow them. Jesus "had compassion for them, because they were like sheep without a shepherd; and he began to teach them many things." Then realizing that they are hungry, Jesus feeds them with five loaves and two fish. Moreover, he has the disciples distribute the loaves and fish, not taking the credit for himself. As you contemplate these two scenes, note the different values that are shown by the actions of Herod and of Jesus.

At the end of the meditation on the Two Standards Ignatius recommends a triple colloquy, one similar to the one we presented in chapter 7. First, I approach Mary and

beg her to obtain for me grace from her Son and Lord that I may be received under his standard; and first, in the most perfect spiritual poverty; and also, if his Divine Majesty should be served and if he should wish to choose me for it, to no less a degree of actual poverty; and second, in bearing reproaches and injuries, that through them I may imitate him more, if only I can do this without sin on anyone's part and without displeasure to the Divine Majesty. Then I will say a Hail Mary (n. 147).

If you can make this prayer, then do so. Then approach Jesus and ask the same grace from him and say the prayer Soul of Christ. (Cf. Appendix A.) Finally ask the same grace from God the Father and say an Our Father. The suggestion of the triple colloquy indicates how important Ignatius thinks it is that we have a deep interior knowledge of the snares of the evil one and of the values of Jesus.

Ignatius adds a further meditation for this "fourth day," a meditation on three classes of people all of whom have come into the possession of a considerable amount of money to which they are attached. They want to do the right thing about the money and to "find God our Lord in peace, by discarding the burden and obstacle to this purpose which this attachment to the acquired money is found to be" (n. 150). The first kind of person would like to get rid of the attachment to the money, but does nothing to get rid of the attachment right up to the hour of his death. The second kind of person also wants to get rid of the attachment, but she does it on her own terms; she will, for example, give some of the money for a worthy project. The third kind of person wants to get rid of the attachment and leaves the decision of what to do about the money entirely up to God; she tries to discern what God wants her to do about the money. Ignatius says that this kind of person

> strives earnestly not to desire that money or anything else, except when one is motivated solely by the service of God our Lord; in such a way that the desire to be able to serve God our Lord better is what moves one to take or reject any object whatsoever (n. 155).

Reflect on these three kinds of people and apply the reflections to yourself. At the end, Ignatius suggests, make the same triple colloquy just described.

Remember to reflect for some moments after each period of prayer. Did you get what you wanted? What most moved you? What left you unmoved? Make some notes for yourself. Such notes, as you are now aware, can be very helpful for repetitions, for discussions with your spiritual director or for sharing with your peer group.

13

"I WANT TO KNOW-LOVE JESUS BETTER AND TO BE HIS DISCIPLE" PART IV

After the time spent meditating and reflecting on the struggle between Jesus and the dark forces opposed to God's intention, your desire now probably is to deepen your knowledge and love of Jesus and to become a close disciple and fellow worker with him. In this chapter I will suggest contemplations from the section of the gospel of Mark that begins with the cure of a blind man in Bethsaida and ends with the cure of the blind Bartimaeus (Mk 8: 22–10: 52). This section is bounded by the cures of the blind men, perhaps a clue to the meaning of the whole section. In between these cures of blindness, Jesus three times predicts his death by crucifixion, and each time the disciples display incomprehension. They do not see the cost of being the Christ (Messiah) or the cost of discipleship. Yet Jesus seems to be trying to teach them both things. Your desire to know and love Jesus better in order to follow him more closely may also encounter resistance as you come to recognize the costs of being close to Jesus. Such resistance is to be expected. If you do encounter such resistance, ask the Lord to help you to overcome it. You might also continue to use the triple colloquy from the last chapter to keep before your mind and heart that you need God's help to perceive how your resistance and the wiles of the evil one are leading you away from your heart's desire.

For the first contemplation I suggest that you use the text of the cure of the blind man in Bethsaida, Mark 8: 22–26. As you begin the period of prayer, remember to say the preparatory prayer described in chapter 1 and then express your desire to the Lord. Then read the text which follows:

> They came to Bethsaida. Some people brought a blind man to him and begged him to touch him. He took the blind man by the hand and led him out of the village; and when he had put saliva on his eyes and laid his hands on him, he asked him, "Can you see anything?" And the man looked up and said, "I can see people, but they look like trees, walking." Then Jesus laid his hands on his eyes again; and he looked intently and his sight was restored, and he saw everything clearly. Then he sent him away to his home, saying, "Do not even go into the village."

Let the text touch your imagination as you have done before. You will probably notice that this kind of contemplation is becoming both easier and harder; easier in that you now have so much experience with this type of prayer; harder because you may be experiencing more subtle resistance to closeness to Jesus. If you do experience some resistance, speak to Jesus about it and ask his help. Notice that the cure of this man's blindness does not come all at once. When you are at the end of your prayer period, say an Our Father (or the triple colloquy) and then take the usual few minutes to reflect on the prayer period and to make some notes for yourself.

For the next contemplation I suggest that you take the next section of the gospel, the confession of Peter, the first prediction of the passion and its aftermath. After the usual preparatory prayer and the expression of your desire, begin to read the text.

> Jesus went on with his disciples to the villages of Caesarea Philippi; and on the way he asked his disciples, "Who do people say that I am?" And they answered him, "John the Baptist; and others, Elijah; and still others, one of the prophets." He asked them, "But who do you say that I am?" Peter answered him, "You are the Messiah." And he sternly ordered them not to tell anyone about him.
> Then he began to teach them that the Son of Man must undergo great suffering, and be rejected by the elders, the chief priests, and the scribes, and be killed, and after three days rise again. He said all this quite openly. And Peter took him aside and began to rebuke him. But turning and looking at his disciples, he rebuked Peter and said, "Get behind me, Satan! For you are setting your mind not on divine things but on human things" (Mk 8: 27–33).

Try to become a part of the scene in your usual way. Do you hear Jesus say to you: "Who do you say that I am?" How do you answer him? How do you react when he predicts his passion? Do you sympathize with Peter? How do you react to Jesus' anger and the strong rebuke of Peter? These are only questions to remind you of some of the things that contemplation of this text might prompt in your mind and heart. Again, at the end of the prayer, end with an Our Father (or the triple colloquy) and then take a few moments for reflection on the prayer period.

For your next two or three periods of prayer (or even more, if you sense that more can be gotten from more repetitions) go back over these two contemplations, especially to those places or moments when you were most moved. You might also want to spend more time contemplating those aspects of the scene that you think should have moved you, but left you unmoved. It is possible that such lack of movement indicates resistance. But don't force anything. If you are resisting a new initiative or revelation of the Lord, that will make itself known soon enough through a general dryness in prayer. Let me remind you once again of the purpose of the repetitions. They are suggested as a way to have you savor and appropriate more deeply the insights and knowledge and love of Jesus that the Lord is revealing to you. Ignatius says: "For what fills and satisfies the soul consists, not in knowing much, but in our understanding the realities profoundly and in savoring them interiorly" (n. 2). These repetitions are also a way to let the Lord help you to overcome resistance to further intimacy with him. At the end of each of the repetitions say an Our Father (or the triple colloquy) and take some time for reflection as usual.

The next time you want to try some new material take the section immediately following the first prediction. Here Jesus speaks openly of the cost of discipleship. Begin with the usual preparatory prayer and the expression of your desire which still is, I presume, to know Jesus more personally in order to love him more intensely and to follow him more closely. Then read the text:

He called the crowd with his disciples, and said to them, "If any want to become my followers, let them deny themselves and take up their cross and follow me. For those who want to save their life will lose it, and those who lose their life for my sake, and for the sake of the gospel, will save it. For what will it profit them to gain the whole world and forfeit their life? Indeed, what can they give in return for their life? Those who are ashamed of me and of my words in this adulterous and sinful generation, of them the Son of Man will also be ashamed when he comes in the glory of his Father with the holy angels" (Mk 8: 34–38).

Try to be one of the people in the crowd as Jesus speaks these words. How do you react to them? Tell Jesus your reactions and listen for some sense of his response to you. Do you still want to follow him more closely? Do you want to, but also sense some fear and hesitation? Remember that relationships deepen through mutual transparency, through the willingness of each party to tell the other the truth about oneself and about one's reactions to the other's statements and actions. Telling Jesus how you feel, even if you feel some revulsion or fear toward him, can only help your relationship with him. At the end of the period say an Our Father (or the triple colloquy) and then take the usual few moments to reflect on the period and to make some notes for yourself.

Next I suggest that you contemplate the transfiguration of Jesus in Mark's gospel. One can look on this event as a transforming experience in Jesus' life which Peter, James and John were privileged to witness, an experience of the presence of God to him that looks back to the experience at his baptism and forward to the experience in the garden of Gethsemane. Begin with the usual preparatory prayer and the expression of your desire. Then read the text and let it touch your imagination.

> Six days later, Jesus took with him Peter and James and John, and led them up a high mountain apart, by themselves. And he was transfigured before them, and his clothes became dazzling white, such as no one on earth could bleach them. And there appeared to them Elijah with Moses, who were talking with Jesus. Then Peter said to Jesus, "Rabbi, it is good for us to be here; let us make three dwellings, one for you, one for Moses, and one for Elijah." He did not know what to say for they were terrified. Then a cloud overshadowed them, and from the cloud there came a voice, "This is my Son, the Beloved; listen to him!" Suddenly when they looked around, they saw

no one with them any more, but only Jesus. As they were coming down the mountain, he ordered them to tell no one about what they had seen, until after the Son of Man had risen from the dead. So they kept the matter to themselves, questioning what this rising from the dead could mean (Mk 9: 2–10).

Moses and Elijah were two of the most important figures in the history of the Israelites; Moses the leader of the exodus and the lawgiver; Elijah the prophet who was taken up into heaven in a fiery chariot and who, it was popularly believed, would return as the harbinger of the Messiah. What were they talking about with Jesus? Luke indicates that they were talking about his coming death and resurrection (Lk 9:31). So this experience comes as Jesus faces his great trial by fire. How do you react as you imagine yourself in the scene? How does Jesus feel as he hears the voice of his Father? How does he feel as he talks with Moses and Elijah about his departure in Jerusalem? How do you feel as you get to know Jesus more intimately? Talk to Jesus as you would to a friend who has just let you into the deepest secrets of his heart. At the end of the prayer end with an Our Father (or the triple colloquy) and then take the usual time for reflection and some notes to yourself.

For the next two or three (or more) periods of prayer do repetitions on these two contemplations, asking Jesus to deepen your knowledge and love of him and your desire to follow him more closely. During this time of a deepening knowledge and love of Jesus you may begin to wonder what shape your life from now on should take. If you are not yet embarked on a particular way of life, for example, a life career, marriage, religious life, you may want to ask the Lord to enlighten you as to how he wants you to shape your life. Reflection on this question and your reactions to

various possible options may give you clarity as to the
direction your life should take. Discussion of your reflections and the movements in your heart and mind with a
spiritual director would be very helpful as you try to discern which of the various movements and reactions of
your heart and mind are from God. If your life already has
a set shape that does not admit of a radical change, you
might be wondering how your new relationship with Jesus
will shape your way of living your life. Again you can talk
this over with Jesus and ask for enlightenment. "What
does following you more closely mean for my present way
of life? Are there any changes in behavior that need to be
made to reflect this new relationship with you?" At the
end of each repetition say an Our Father (or the triple colloquy) and take time for the usual reflection on the prayer
period.

For new material after this you can continue with the
various scenes of Mark's gospel, using two new texts and
then making repetitions as has been the pattern up to
now. For the sake of brevity I want to suggest only two
more sets of new material in this chapter. The first set
begins with the second prediction of the passion and is
followed by the story of the rich young man. Begin with
the usual preparatory prayer and then express your desire.
Then read the text contemplatively.

> They went on from there and passed through Galilee. He
> did not want anyone to know it; for he was teaching his dis-
> ciples, saying to them, "The Son Man is to be betrayed into
> human hands, and they will kill him, and three days after
> being killed, he will rise again." But they did not under-
> stand what he was saying and were afraid to ask him.
>   Then they came to Capernaum; and when he was in the
> house he asked them, "What were you arguing about on
> the way?" But they were silent, for on the way they had

argued with one another who was the greatest. He sat down, called the twelve, and said to them, "Whoever wants to be first must be last of all and servant of all." Then he took a little child and put it among them; and taking it in his arms, he said to them, "Whoever welcomes one such child in my name welcomes me, and whoever welcomes me welcomes not me but the one who sent me" (Mk 9: 30-37).

Let your imagination work with this scene in the usual way. Speak to Jesus about whatever comes to your mind and heart; take time to listen for some indication of his response to you. If you have any questions or reactions about your own way of life, make them known to Jesus. By this time you should have much practice in such contemplation and much knowledge of how Jesus and you interact. End the prayer period with an Our Father (or the triple colloquy) and take the usual time to reflect and to take some notes for yourself.

For the next period of prayer I suggest the text about the rich young man. Begin with the usual preparatory prayer and express your desire. Then read the text contemplatively.

As he was setting out on a journey, a man ran up and knelt before him, and asked him, "Good Teacher, what must I do to inherit eternal life?" Jesus said to him, "Why do you call me good? No one is good but God alone. You know the commandments: "You shall not murder; You shall not commit adultery; You shall not steal; You shall not bear false witness; You shall not defraud; Honor your father and mother.'" He said to him, "Teacher, I have kept all these since my youth." Jesus, looking at him, loved him and said, "You lack one thing; go, sell what you own, and give the money to the poor, and you will have treasure in heaven; then come, follow me." When he heard this, he was

shocked and went away grieving, for he had many possessions (Mk 10: 17–22).

Use your imagination in the usual way and say to Jesus
whatever occurs to you. Notice that the young man goes
away grieving; his inordinate attachment to his wealth will
not let him have his deepest desire, intimate friendship
with Jesus. End the prayer period with an Our Father and
take some time for the usual reflection and notetaking.
For your next two or three (or more) prayer periods do
repetitions of these two contemplations in the usual way.

The second set of new material begins with the third
prediction of the passion and is followed by the cure of
the blind man Bartimaeus. As you begin your period of
prayer say the usual preparatory prayer and then express
your desire. Then read the text contemplatively.

They were on the road, going up to Jerusalem, and Jesus
was walking ahead of them; they were amazed, and those
who followed were afraid. He took the twelve aside again
and began to tell them what was to happen to him, saying,
"See, we are going up to Jerusalem, and the Son of Man
will be handed over to the chief priests and the scribes,
and they will condemn him to death; then they will hand
him over to the Gentiles; they will mock him, and spit
upon him, and flog him, and kill him; and after three days
he will rise again."

James and John, the sons of Zebedee, came forward to
him and said to him, "Teacher, we want you to do for us
whatever we ask of you." And he said to them, "What is it
you want me to do for you?" And they said to him, "Grant
us to sit, one at your right hand and one at your left, in
your glory." But Jesus said to them, "You do not know
what you are asking. Are you able to drink the cup that I
drink, or be baptized with the baptism that I am baptized
with?" They replied, "We are able." Then Jesus said to

them, "The cup that I drink you will drink; and with the baptism with which I am baptized, you will be baptized; but to sit at my right hand or at my left is not mine to grant, but it is for those for whom it has been prepared."

When the ten heard this, they began to be angry with James and John. So Jesus called them and said to them, "You know that among the Gentiles those whom they recognize as their rulers lord it over them, and their great ones are tyrants over them. But it is not so among you; but whoever wishes to become great among you must be your servant, and whoever wishes to be first among you must be slave of all. For the Son of Man came not to be served but to serve, and to give his life a ransom for many" (Mk 10: 32–45).

Use your imagination in the usual way. Recall the value system of Christ and of Satan from the meditation on The Two Standards. Speak to Jesus as you would to a friend and ask him to respond to you. Take time to be quiet so that he will have a chance to communicate to you in the way to which you have become accustomed. End the prayer period with an Our Father (or the triple colloquy) and then take the usual time for reflection and notetaking.

For the second prayer period of this set take the story of the cure of Bartimaeus, which ends this section that began with the cure of the blind man in Bethsaida. Begin with the usual preparatory prayer and then express your desire. Read the text contemplatively.

They came to Jericho. As he and his disciples and a large crowd were leaving Jericho, Bartimaeus son of Timaeus, a blind beggar, was sitting by the roadside. When he heard that it was Jesus of Nazareth, he began to shout and say, "Jesus, Son of David, have mercy on me!" Many sternly ordered him to be quiet, but he cried out even more loudly, "Son of David, have mercy on me!" Jesus stood still and

said, "Call him here." And they called the blind man, saying to him, "Take heart; get up, he is calling you." So
throwing off his cloak, he sprang up and came to Jesus.
Then Jesus said to him, "What do you want me to do for
you?" The blind man said to him, "My teacher, let me see
again." Jesus said to him, "Go; your faith has made you
well." Immediately he regained his sight and followed him
on the way (Mk 10: 46–52).

Use your imagination in the usual way. Let me just remind
you of two things. When the blind man in Bethsaida was
cured, he was not allowed to follow Jesus; he was sent
home. Now Bartimaeus follows Jesus "on the way." Moreover, the way is the "way of the cross," since with the very
next verse Jesus enters Jerusalem for the last week of his
life. Also, the early Christians were called the "people of
the way." These reminders may help your contemplation
of this passage. End your prayer period with an Our
Father (or the triple colloquy) and make the usual reflection. For the next two or three (or more) prayer periods
do repetitions of these two contemplations. You may be
concerned at this time about the future shape of your life
in the context of this new relationship with Jesus. Bring
this topic into your talks with Jesus.

If you want to continue contemplating the public life of
Jesus in Mark's gospel, you can use the same method we
have been suggesting with chapters 11 through 13, taking
two new scenes and then making two or three or more
repetitions before taking two other scenes. In fact, you can
use this method with another gospel if you want to. We
will never get to know enough about Jesus in a lifetime—
nor even in eternity.

14

"I WANT TO SHARE JESUS' SUFFERING"

Whenever you love someone, you open yourself up to the pain of loss when your loved one gets ill, suffers pain and/or dies. It can be very difficult to share a loved one's pain and dying. Still at our best we do want to be with a loved one and to share the pain and all the emotions that go with the approach of death. In Frederick Buechner's novel *Lion Country* the narrator, Antonio, is speaking of his sister Miriam's dying of a very painful bone cancer.

> When Miriam's bones were breaking, for instance, if I could have pushed a button that would have stopped not her pain but the pain of her pain in me, I would not have pushed the button because, to put it quite simply, my pain was because I loved her, and to have wished my pain away would have been somehow to wish my love away as well. And at my best and bravest I do not want to escape the future either, even though I know that it contains what will someday be my own great and final pain. Because a distaste for dying is twin to a taste for living, and again I don't think you can tamper with one without somehow doing mischief to the other. But this is at my best and bravest. The rest of the time I am a fool and a coward (242).

At our best and bravest we do want to share the pain of our loved one.

However, the loved one has to cooperate, has to be willing to reveal his or her real experiences, emotions, and thoughts. Often two people who love one another try to spare one another pain when one of them is dying. The one who is dying does not want to cause the beloved pain by revealing how bad it is; the other is afraid to make matters worse by referring to the imminence of death. As a result, the two of them are more lonely and distant from one another than they would want during this final stage of their earthly relationship. If we want our close relationships to continue to grow even through the pain of illness and death, then we have to take the risks of continuing to be mutually transparent with one another. The same is true of our relationship with Jesus.

The closer you come to Jesus the more you may develop a desire to share with Jesus in his suffering and death. Here the desire is that Jesus reveal to you his inner state as he went through the passion and crucifixion so that you can have compassion for him. Ignatius puts the desire this way: "to ask for sorrow, regret, and confusion, because the Lord is going to his Passion for my sins" (n. 193). The focus of this desire is Jesus' own experience of this horrible death; you want Jesus to reveal himself to you so that you can suffer with (have compassion for) him. If you have this desire, then the exercises in this chapter may help you to let Jesus fulfill your desire.

The first period of prayer will be a contemplation of the last supper. Begin with the usual preparatory prayer and then express your desire. Then read the text contemplatively. I will continue with the gospel of Mark, but you can use the passion story in any of the gospels.

When it was evening (of the first day of Passover), he came with the twelve (to the upper room). And when they had taken their places and were eating, Jesus said, "Truly I tell

you, one of you will betray me, one who is eating with me."
They began to be distressed and to say to him one after
another, "Surely, not I?" He said to them, "It is one of the
twelve, one who is dipping bread into the bowl with me.
For the Son of Man goes as it is written of him, but woe to
that one by whom the Son Man is betrayed! It would have
been better for that one not to have been born."

While they were eating, he took a loaf of bread, and
after blessing it he broke it, gave it to them, and said,
"Take; this is my body." Then he took a cup, and after giving thanks he gave it to them, and all of them drank from
it. He said to them, "This is my blood of the covenant,
which is poured out for many. Truly I tell you, I will never
again drink of the fruit of the vine until that day when I
drink it new in the kingdom of God."

When they had sung the hymn, they went out to the
Mount of Olives. And Jesus said to them, "You will all
become deserters; for it is written, "I will strike the shepherd, and the sheep will be scattered.' But after I am raised
up, I will go before you to Galilee." Peter said to him,
"Even though all become deserters, I will not." Jesus said to
him, "Truly I tell you, this day, this very night, before the
cock crows twice, you will deny me three times." But he
said vehemently, " Even though I must die with you, I will
not deny you." And all of them said the same (Mk 14:
17-31).

Let this text stir your imagination. Do you sense the atmosphere in the room? How do the apostles react to Jesus'
announcement? Does Jesus let you know his emotions and
reactions as he hears each of them, including Judas, ask
"Surely, not I?" What are your own feelings as you take in
the scene? Does Judas receive the bread and the cup along
with the others? I ask these questions only to help prime
the pump. Your own imagination will take over as you let
the text work on you. Continue to ask Jesus to reveal himself to you. If you feel any reluctance to continue the con-

templation, let Jesus know and ask for his help to stay with him through this painful time. As you end the period of prayer say an Our Father. You could, if it helps, pray to Mary to intercede for you to obtain what you want from her Son, and then approach Jesus himself, and finally the Father. Then take some time for reflection on the period and to make some notes for yourself.

The second contemplation will be of the events in Gethsemane. Begin with the usual preparatory prayer and then express your desire. The text follows:

> They went to a place called Gethsemane; and he said to his disciples, "Sit here while I pray." He took with him Peter and James and John, and began to be distressed and agitated. And he said to them, " I am deeply grieved, even to death; remain here, and keep awake." And going a little farther, he threw himself on the ground and prayed that, if it were possible, the hour might pass from him. He said, "Abba, Father, for you all things are possible; remove this cup from me; yet, not what I want, but what you want." He came and found them sleeping; and he said to Peter, "Simon, are you asleep? Could you not keep awake one hour? Keep awake and pray that you may not come into the time of trial; the spirit indeed is willing, but the flesh is weak." And again he went away and prayed, saying the same words. And once more he came and found them sleeping, for their eyes were very heavy; and they did not know what to say to him. He came a third time and said to them, "Are you still sleeping and taking your rest? Enough! The hour has come; the Son of Man is betrayed into the hands of sinners. Get up, let us be going. See, my betrayer is at hand."

> Immediately, while he was still speaking, Judas, one of the twelve, arrived; and with him there was a crowd with swords and clubs, from the chief priests, the scribes, and the elders. Now the betrayer had given them a sign, saying, "The one I will kiss is the man; arrest him and lead him

away under guard." So when he came, he went up to him at once and said, "Rabbi!" and kissed him. Then they laid hands on him and arrested him. But one of those who stood near drew his sword and struck the slave of the high priest, cutting off his ear. Then Jesus said to them, "Have you come out with swords and clubs to arrest me as though I were a bandit? Day after day I was with you in the temple teaching, and you did not arrest me. But let the scriptures be fulfilled." All of them deserted him and fled (Mk 14: 32–50).

Let the text work on your imagination as usual. Let me remind you that Peter, James and John were also witnesses of the transfiguration. They find it very difficult to witness this agony. You, too, may find it difficult. It is only to be expected that we want to turn our eyes away, or fall asleep, before such suffering in one whom we now love so much. If you do experience reluctance or resistance, let Jesus know and ask his help. The reluctance is not the only motive operative in you; you also really do desire to suffer with Jesus, to remain awake with him. At the end say an Our Father (or a triple colloquy) and then take time for reflection and notetaking. For your next two or three or more periods of prayer go back over these two contemplations in the usual manner.

For the next two periods of prayer take first the scene of Jesus' trial before the high priest, Mark 14: 53–65. After the usual preparatory prayer tell the Lord your desire. Then read the text contemplatively.

They took Jesus to the high priest; and all the chief priests, the elders, and the scribes were assembled. Peter had followed him at a distance, right into the courtyard of the high priest; and he was sitting with the guards, warming himself at the fire. Now the chief priests and the whole council were looking for testimony against Jesus to put him to death; but they found none. For many gave false testimony against him, and their testimony did not agree. Some stood up and gave false testimony against him, saying, "We heard him say, 'I will destroy this temple that is made with hands, and in three days I will build another, not made with hands.'" But even on this point their testimony did not agree. Then the high priest stood up before them and asked Jesus, "Have you no answer? What is it that they testify against you?" But he was silent and did not answer. Again the high priest asked him, "Are you the Messiah, the Son of the Blessed One?" Jesus said, "I am; and "you will see the Son of Man seated at the right hand of the Power, and "coming with the clouds of heaven." Then the high priest tore his clothes and said, "Why do we still need witnesses? You have heard his blasphemy! What is your decision?" All of them condemned him as deserving death. Some began to spit on him, to blindfold him and to strike him, saying to him, "Prophesy!" The guards also took him over and beat him.

Use the scene imaginatively in your usual manner. End with an Our Father (or a triple colloquy) and take the usual time for reflection.

For your second period take the scene of Peter's denial, Mark 14: 66–72. After the usual preparatory prayer tell Jesus what you desire and then read the text contemplatively.

While Peter was below in the courtyard, one of the servant-girls of the high priest came by. When she saw Peter warming himself, she stared at him and said, "You also were with Jesus, the man from Nazareth." But he denied it, saying, "I do not know or understand what you are talking about." And he went out into the forecourt. Then the cock crowed. And the servant-girl, on seeing him, began again to say to the bystanders, "This man is one of them." But again he denied it. Then after a little while the bystanders again said to Peter, "Certainly you are one of them; for you are a Galilean." But he began to curse, and he swore an oath, "I do not know this man you are talking about." At that moment the cock crowed for the second time. Then Peter remembered that Jesus had said to him, "Before the cock crows twice, you will deny me three times." And he broke down and wept.

Again end the prayer period with an Our Father and the usual time of reflection. For the next two or more periods of prayer go back over these last two scenes.

For the next two periods of prayer take first the trial before Pilate, Mark 15: 1–15. After the usual preparatory prayer and the expression of your desire read the text contemplatively and speak with Jesus and listen to him.

As soon as it was morning, the chief priests held a consultation with the elders and scribes and the whole council. They bound Jesus, led him away, and handed him over to Pilate. Pilate asked him, "Are you the King of the Jews?" He answered him, "You say so." Then the chief priests accused him of many things. Pilate asked him again, "Have you no answer? See how many charges they bring against you." But Jesus made no further reply, so that Pilate was amazed. Now at the festival he used to release a prisoner for them, anyone for whom they asked. Now a man called Barabbas was in prison with the rebels who had committed murder during the insurrection. So the crowd came and began to ask Pilate to do for them according to his custom. Then he answered them, "Do you want me to release for you the King of the Jews?" For he realized that it was out of jealousy that the chief priests had handed him over. But the chief priests stirred up the crowd to have him release Barabbas for them instead. Pilate spoke to them again, "Then what do you wish me to do with the man you call the King of the Jews?" They shouted back, "Crucify him!" Pilate asked them, "Why, what evil has he done?" But they shouted all the more, "Crucify him!" So Pilate, wishing to satisfy the crowd, released Barabbas for them; and after flogging Jesus, he handed him over to be crucified.

You might note that Pilate does something that he does not want to do and recall the meditation on the Two Standards. End the prayer period with an Our Father (or a triple colloquy) and take some time for reflection as usual.

For your next period of prayer take the crowning with thorns and mocking, Mark 15:16–20. After the usual preparatory prayer and expression of your desire read the text contemplatively and continue your dialogue with Jesus and Mary and anyone else.

> Then the soldiers led him into the courtyard of the palace (that is, the governor's headquarters); and they called together the whole cohort. And they clothed him in a purple cloak; and after twisting some thorns into a crown, they put it on him. And they began saluting him, "Hail, King of the Jews!" They struck his head with a reed, spat upon him, and knelt down in homage to him. After mocking him, they stripped him of the purple cloak and put his own clothes on him. Then they led him out to crucify him.

After you have finished the contemplation of this scene, end the period with an Our Father (or a triple colloquy) and take the usual time for reflection. Follow these two periods of prayer with two or more repetitions as usual.

Next you can take first the way of the cross to Golgotha and the nailing to the cross, Mark 15: 21–32. After the usual preparatory prayer and the expression of your desire, read the text contemplatively and continue your dialogue with Jesus, Mary and any others.

> They compelled a passer-by, who was coming in from the country, to carry his cross; it was Simon of Cyrene, the

father of Alexander and Rufus. Then they brought Jesus to the place called Golgotha (which means the place of a skull). And they offered him wine mixed with myrrh; but he did not take it. And they crucified him, and divided his clothes among them, casting lots to decide what each should take. It was nine o'clock in the morning when they crucified him. The inscription of the charge against him read, "The King of the Jews." And with him they crucified two bandits, one on his right and one on his left. Those who passed by derided him, shaking their heads and saying, "Aha! You who would destroy the temple and build it in three days, save yourself, and come down from the cross!" In the same way the chief priests, along with the scribes, were also mocking him among themselves and saying, "He saved others; he cannot save himself. Let the Messiah, the King of Israel, come down from the cross now, so that we may see and believe." Those who were crucified with him also taunted him.

End your prayer period in the usual way.

For your next period of prayer take the final hours on the cross until the death of Jesus, Mark 15: 33–41. After the usual preparatory prayer and the expression of your wish, read the text contemplatively and continue your dialogue with Jesus and Mary and others.

When it was noon, darkness came over the whole land until three in the afternoon. At three o'clock Jesus cried out with a loud voice, "Eloi, Eloi, lema sabachthani?" which means, "My God, my God, why have you forsaken me?" When some of the bystanders heard it, they said, "Listen, he is calling for Elijah." And someone ran, filled a sponge with sour wine, put it on a stick, and gave it to him to drink, saying, "Wait, let us see whether Elijah will come to take him down." Then Jesus gave a loud cry and breathed his last. And the curtain of the temple was torn in two, from top to bottom. Now when the centurion, who stood facing him, saw that in this way he breathed his last, he said, "Truly this man was God's Son!" There were also women looking on from a distance; among them were Mary Magdalene, and Mary the mother of James the younger and of Joses, and Salome. These used to follow him and provided for him when he was in Galilee; and there were many other women who had come up with him to Jerusalem.

End your period of prayer in the usual way. Follow these two periods with the usual repetitions.

You can take longer to go through the passion and death, of course. You can also use scenes from the other gospels as well. Once you have gone step-by-step through the whole passion, then, as Ignatius suggests, take a couple of periods of prayer to contemplate the whole passion in one setting. Remember that you are asking Jesus to reveal himself to you. This may take some time, both because Jesus is free to reveal himself or not and because you may consciously or unconsciously resist the revelation. You might also remember that it could take years of growing in the knowledge and love of Jesus before, by the grace of God, you experience the full depths of Jesus' suffering.

15

"I WANT TO SHARE JESUS' PRESENT JOY"

"If Christ has not been raised, your faith is futile and you are still in your sins....If for this life only we have hoped in Christ, we are of all people most to be pitied" (1 Cor 15: 17–19). These words of St. Paul remind us that the life and death of Jesus Christ would have no meaning for any of us if he were not raised from the dead. Our faith tells us that Jesus is still alive. Moreover, your own experience of Jesus as you have made your way through this book testifies that Jesus lives and is still vitally interested in you and in all of his brothers and sisters. Now that you have compassionately shared in the passion and death of Jesus, perhaps you desire to share in the joy of his resurrection. Ignatius puts the desire at this point in this way: "to ask for the grace to be glad and to rejoice intensely because of the great glory and joy of Christ our Lord" (n. 221). Note that the desire is to be glad most of all for Jesus' sake, but since mutuality of friendship is involved, the joy is also for yourself, that the one whom you love is still alive. If this is your desire, then you might want to try out the exercises of this chapter.

For the first period of prayer Ignatius suggests a contemplation of Jesus' appearance to his mother, Mary. There is no biblical text of such an appearance. But we can piously presume that Jesus first appeared to his mother who had suffered with him by standing at the cross until he died. If you are so inclined, you might want to try such a contemplation. Begin with the usual preparatory prayer and then express your desire that Jesus reveal to you his own exaltation and joy and let you share in it. Then imagine Jesus appearing to Mary. How do they look at one another? What do they say? What do they do? We will see in the later contemplations that Jesus is at first not recognized when he appears. Is that the case with Mary? Ignatius indicates that during the resurrection appearances Jesus acts as consoler to his mother and to his friends. Do you experience him as acting in this way with you? Engage in dialogue with Jesus and with Mary in whatever way suits you. End the prayer period with an Our Father and then take the usual time for reflection and notetaking.

The gospel of Mark has very little on the resurrection. In fact, some manuscripts indicate doubt about the authenticity of the section from 16: 9 to the end of the gospel. For your contemplations of the resurrection appearances, you will be better served by using scenes from the gospels of Luke and John. I will suggest three scenes here, but by now you know the method of contemplation according to Ignatius well enough so that you can move along on your own. Remember to do repetitions of the contemplations that move you most deeply. Also remember that you are asking for a grace, a personal revelation of Jesus, not something that is in your power to attain on your own. It may take some time before this grace is given. To receive the grace of the joy of the resurrection we must accept the full reality of the horror of the crucifixion. Jesus, glorified, still bears the marks of that horror in his hands, feet and side. Resurrection does not mean that the past is undone; it does mean that the horror and the death are not the whole story. At any rate, be patient with yourself as you contem-

plate these resurrection scenes and keep insisting with
Jesus that you want to share in his joy.

Let me suggest a contemplation of the appearance to
Mary Magdalene as recorded in the gospel of John. Begin
with the usual preparatory prayer and then express your
desire. Then read the text contemplatively.

> But Mary stood weeping outside the tomb. As she wept,
> she bent over to look into the tomb; and she saw two
> angels in white, sitting where the body of Jesus had been
> lying, one at the head and the other at the feet. They said
> to her, "Woman, why are you weeping?" She said to them,
> "They have taken away my Lord, and I do not know where
> they have laid him." When she had said this, she turned
> around and saw Jesus standing there, but she did not know
> that it was Jesus. Jesus said to her, "Woman, why are you
> weeping? Whom are you looking for?" Supposing him to
> be the gardener, she said to him, "Sir, if you have carried
> him away, tell me where you have laid him, and I will take
> him away." Jesus said to her, "Mary!" She turned and said
> to him in Hebrew, "Rabbouni!" (which means Teacher).
> Jesus said to her, "Do not hold on to me, because I have
> not yet ascended to the Father. But go to my brothers and
> say to them, 'I am ascending to my Father and your Father,
> to my God and your God.'" Mary Magdalene went and
> announced to the disciples, "I have seen the Lord"; and she
> told them that he had said these things to her (Jn 20:
> 11–18).

Let these words work on your imagination in the usual
way. Note that Mary does not recognize Jesus at first. But
the sound of her own name touches something deep in
her, and she instantly recognizes that she is face-to-face
with her beloved Jesus. What are your reactions? What do
you want to happen to you? What do you want Jesus to tell
you about his experiences? Engage in dialogue with Jesus.

At the end of the prayer period say an Our Father and take the usual time for reflection and notetaking.

Next I suggest a contemplation of Jesus' appearance to the disciples as described in the following section of John's gospel. Begin with the usual preparatory prayer and then express your desire for this period of prayer. Then read the text contemplatively.

> When it was evening on that day, the first day of the week, and the doors of the house where the disciples had met were locked for fear of the Jews, Jesus came and stood among them and said, "Peace be with you." After he said this, he showed them his hands and his side. Then the disciples rejoiced when they saw the Lord. Jesus said to them again, "Peace be with you. As the Father has sent me, so I send you." When he had said this, he breathed on them and said to them, "Receive the Holy Spirit. If you forgive the sins of any, they are forgiven them; if you retain the sins of any, they are retained" (Jn 20: 19–23).

Imagine the disciples huddled together in this locked room, afraid. How do they feel? What are they saying to one another? Do they trust one another, do you think? Suddenly into their midst comes Jesus. He still has the wounds of the crucifixion, but he brings joy and hope to them. The word for breath in Hebrew is also translated as wind or as spirit. Jesus' act of breathing on the disciples is a reminder of the Spirit of God hovering over creation in the first chapter of the book of Genesis. The author of the gospel is alluding to a new creation in this scene. How do you react? Are you experiencing Jesus as a consoler for you? Are you beginning to share in the joy of his resurrection? Speak to him and listen to him. End the prayer period in the usual way with an Our Father and time for reflection. You might want to do a repetition or two in the prayer periods that follow the contemplation of two resurrection scenes.

Finally I want to suggest the appearance of Jesus to the two disciples who were on the road to Emmaus. Begin with the usual preparatory prayer and then express your desire. Now read the text contemplatively.

Now on that same day two of them were going to a village called Emmaus, about seven miles from Jerusalem, and talking with each other about all these things that had happened. While they were talking and discussing, Jesus himself came near and went with them, but their eyes were kept from recognizing him. And he said to them, "What are you discussing with each other while you walk along?" They stood still, looking sad. Then one of them, whose name was Cleopas, answered him, "Are you the only stranger in Jerusalem who does not know the things that have taken place there in these days?" He asked them, "What things?" They replied, "The things about Jesus of Nazareth, who was a prophet mighty in deed and word before God and all the people, and how our chief priests and leaders handed him over to be condemned to death and crucified him. But we had hoped that he was the one to redeem Israel. Yes, and besides all this, it is now the third day since these things took place. Moreover, some women of our group astounded us. They were at the tomb early this morning, and when they did not find his body there, they came back and told us that they had indeed seen a vision of angels who said that he was alive. Some of those who were with us went to the tomb and found it just as the women had said; but they did not see him." Then he said to them, "Oh, how foolish you are, and how slow of heart to believe all that the prophets have declared! Was it not necessary that the Messiah should suffer these things and then enter into his glory?" Then beginning with Moses and all the prophets, he interpreted to them the things about himself in all the scriptures.
As they came near the village to which they were going, he walked ahead as if he were going on. But they urged him

strongly, saying, "Stay with us, because it is almost evening and day is now nearly over." So he went in to stay with them. When he was at the table with them, he took bread, blessed and broke it, and gave it to them. Then their eyes were opened, and they recognized him; and he vanished from their sight. They said to each other, "Were not our hearts burning within us while he was talking to us on the road, while he was opening the scriptures to us?" That same hour they got up and returned to Jerusalem; and they found the eleven and their companions gathered together. They were saying, "The Lord has risen indeed, and he has appeared to Simon!" Then they told what had happened on the road, and how he had been made known to them in the breaking of the bread (Lk 24: 13–35).

This is a wonderful story to contemplate. Once again the disciples do not recognize him until he makes a characteristic gesture, breaking the bread. Moreover, Jesus tells them that he *had to* suffer and die. Jesus would not be the Messiah he now is if he had not been crucified. The marks of his whole life, including the crucifixion, are part of who he now is in his glorified state. Walk along with them and listen to Jesus, look at him, ask him any questions you want. The disciples were so captivated by this stranger that they did not want to let him go; they prevail on him to stay for supper. Have you ever felt like this with someone you have just met? Felt that you wanted to stay with that person as long as possible? Only upon reflection, perhaps, did you recognize how attracted you were to the person. Then you have some idea of what was going on in these two people. How do you react as you walk along with Jesus? Are you getting what you want? Speak to Jesus as a friend speaks to a friend, and take time to listen for his response. End the prayer period in the usual way with an Our Father and the usual time for reflection.

In this same way you can contemplate all the resurrection appearances in the gospels of Luke and John. You can do this as long as you have the desire to share the joy of the resurrection with Jesus.

16

"I WANT TO LOVE AND SERVE GOD IN ALL THINGS"

The last exercise in the *Spiritual Exercises* is called the contemplation to attain love. The desire Ignatius presumes is a desire "for interior knowledge of all the great good I have received, in order that, stirred to profound gratitude, I may become able to love and serve the Divine Majesty in all things" (n. 233). One of the key phrases in Ignatian spirituality is "finding God in all things." This means to discover God not only in personal or communal prayer, but also at work, play, conversation, indeed, everywhere and at all times. In truth, God as creator and redeemer, we believe, constantly creates us and the whole universe, constantly calls us into community with God the three Persons and with one another, constantly touches each of our hearts with personal revelations of love. Hence, at any moment of our day we are in touch with God. But of course, we are not constantly aware of God's presence. This contemplation is offered by Ignatius to anyone who wants to become more and more aware of God's constant presence and love. Perhaps you have this desire or, at least, desire to have this desire. Then this chapter may help you to let God grant you your desire. Ignatius makes two preliminary observations:

First. Love ought to manifest itself more by deeds than by words.

Second. Love consists in a mutual communication between the two persons. That is, the one who loves gives and communicates to the beloved what he or she has, or a part of what one has or can have; and the beloved in return does the same to the lover. Thus, if the one has knowledge, one gives it to the other who does not; and similarly in regard to honors or riches. Each shares with the other (n. 230–231).

With the first observation Ignatius does not deprecate the expression of one's love for another; rather, he rightly acknowledges that words alone do not prove love. The second observation contains a mind-boggling idea when applied to God, namely that God wants mutuality, that God wants something from each of us human beings. What can we give to God? What does God need? If God is God, then God needs nothing, lacks nothing. However, God freely decides to want something when God creates persons called to enter into the community life of the Trinity. In order to be the God God wants to be for us, we must respond to the call to intimate union.

Recently I had an insight that may illustrate what I mean. In the book of Exodus Moses meets God in the burning bush. God wants Moses to go down to Egypt and free the Israelites. This dialogue takes place.

But Moses said to God, "If I come to the Israelites and say to them, 'The God of your ancestors has sent me to you,' and they ask me, 'What is his name?' what shall I say to them?" God said to Moses, 'I AM WHO I AM." He said further, "Thus you shall say to the Israelites, "I AM has sent me to you.'" God also said to Moses, "Thus you shall say to the Israelites, "THE LORD, the God of your ancestors, the God of Abraham, the God of Isaac, and the God of Jacob, has sent me to you': This is my name forever, and this my title for all generations" (Exod 3: 13–15).

The title "I AM WHO I AM" implies no relations; God just is. But God freely decides to be in relationship with people; I AM becomes the God of Abraham, the God of Isaac, the God of Jacob, the God of Israel, the Father of Jesus Christ, the Father of each one of us human beings. God wants our love and friendship; God cannot have what God wants unless we freely give of ourselves. By free choice God becomes dependent on our response in order to be who God wants to be. That is mind-boggling, isn't it? Do you want to give God what God wants of you? To be more aware of God's presence in your life at every moment? Then this contemplation can help.

Now to the contemplation itself. Begin with the usual preparatory prayer and then express your desire for such an interior knowledge of God's goodness that you will become able to love and serve God in all things. Ignatius suggests four points. Remember that this is a contemplation, not a meditation. You want to experience God as present, not just arrive at this conclusion through reasoning.

The First Point. I will call back into my memory the gifts I have received—my creation, redemption, and other gifts particular to myself. I will ponder with deep affection how much God our Lord has done for me, and how much he has given me of what he possesses, and consequently how he, the same Lord, desires to give me even his very self, in accordance with his divine design.

Then I will reflect on myself, and consider what I on my part ought in all reason and justice to offer and give to the Divine Majesty, namely, all my possessions, and myself along with them. I will speak as one making an offering with deep affection, and say:

"Take, Lord, and receive all my liberty, my memory, my understanding, and all my will—all that I have and possess. You, Lord, have given all that to me. I now give it back to you, O Lord. All of it is yours. Dispose of it according to your will. Give me love of yourself along with your grace, for that is enough for me" (n. 234).

Let your memory bring up all the gifts you have received in your lifetime, all the gifts you have received as you prayed your way through this book. Ask God to let you see the hand of God in all these gifts. See whether you can say—and mean—the prayer suggested by Ignatius. You might recall that "all that I have and possess" includes my thoughts, feelings, reactions, and that intimacy is enhanced by mutual transparency, by the willingness of each person to reveal as much as possible of oneself to the other.

The Second Point. I will consider how God dwells in creatures; in the elements, giving them existence; in the plants, giving them life; in the animals, giving them sensation; in human beings, giving them intelligence; and finally, how in this way he dwells also in myself, giving me existence, life, sensation, and intelligence; and even further, making me his temple, since I am created as a likeness and image of the Divine Majesty. Then once again I will reflect on myself, in the manner described in the first point, or in any other way I feel to be better. This same procedure will be used in each of the following points (n. 235).

Here you are asking to experience the sacredness of the universe and of yourself. If we could experience God's presence in all things in this way, we would be contemplatives in action, people who find God in all things, and we would reverence the environment and all we encounter.

The Third Point. I will consider how God labors and works for me in all the creatures on the face of the earth; that is, he acts in the manner of one who is laboring. For example, he is working in the heavens, elements, plants, fruits, cattle, and all the rest—giving them their existence, conserving them, concurring with their vegetative and sensitive activities, and so forth. Then I will reflect on myself (n. 236).

As you continue in this contemplation, you will probably realize that the Principle and Foundation of chapter 4 is recapitulated in it. In this point we are asking to experience how God creates all the other things in the universe so that we can attain union with God. God is creating the universe so that we can be drawn into the community life of the Trinity.

The Fourth Point. I will consider how all good things and gifts descend from above; for example, my limited power from the Supreme and Infinite Power above; and so of justice, goodness, piety, mercy, and so forth—just as the rays come down from the sun, or the rains from their source. Then I will finish by reflecting on myself, as has been explained. I will conclude with a colloquy and an Our Father (n. 237).

Here we want to experience how all the gifts we have received descend from God. If we could experience just a little how showered we are with God's blessings, then we would be profoundly grateful and humble. We would want to use every gift we have with gratitude, with humility, with profound respect. Moreover, we would know deep in our bones, as it were, that none of these created gifts, no matter how precious, is the object of our deepest desire. Only the Mystery who is the Giver of these gifts answers that desire.

APPENDIX A
PRAYERS

THE HAIL MARY

Hail Mary, full of grace, the Lord is with you. Blessed are you among women. Blessed is the fruit of your womb, Jesus. Holy Mary, Mother of God, pray for us sinners now and at the hour of our death. Amen.

SOUL OF CHRIST

Soul of Christ, sanctify me.
Body of Christ, save me.
Blood of Christ, inebriate me.
Water from the side of Christ, wash me.
Passion of Christ, strengthen me.
O good Jesus, hear me.
Within your wounds hide me.
Do not allow me to be separated from you.
From the malevolent enemy defend me.
In the hour of my death call me,
and bid me come to you,
that with your saints I may praise you
forever and ever. Amen.

APPENDIX B
"HOW CAN I KNOW IT'S GOD COMMUNICATING?" SOME SIMPLE RULES OF THUMB FOR DISCERNMENT

In the *Spiritual Exercises* Ignatius has an appendix called "Rules for the Discernment of Spirits." He says that they are "rules to aid us toward perceiving and then understanding, at least to some extent, the various motions which are caused in the soul: the good motions that they may be received, and the bad that they may be rejected" (n. 313). In this appendix I want to present some rules of thumb based on what Ignatius says that may assist you to make sense of some of the interior movements of your mind, heart and body that occur when you engage in dialogue with the Lord.

Let me say immediately that these rules of thumb are of a rather general kind; at times you will need the help of a spiritual director or of your peer group to help you to sort out what is really happening in your heart. There is always the danger of self-delusion in the matter of developing one's relationship with God. However, I also believe that some spiritual masters have made the discernment of spirits seem more esoteric and difficult than is the case. Ignatius himself began to discern the spirits when he was a spiritual infant and theologically illiterate.

The best way to start, therefore, might be to tell the story of Ignatius' first discernment of spirits. Growing up, he was, by his own admission, something of a hell-raiser. Though destined for the clerical state by his father (he had received the tonsure), he spent his youth and young adulthood pursuing a career as a courtier and warrior. He was also a womanizer. In the battle of Pamplona his legs were badly wounded by a cannonball. Brought back to the castle at Loyola he suffered great pains in order to have his bad leg straightened so that he could still cut a fine figure as a soldier and courtier. During his convalescence the only books available were a life of Christ and a book of the lives of saints. This reading caused him to begin to daydream about following Christ as had St. Francis of Assisi and St. Dominic. He dreamt of living and dying in the Holy Land working for Christ. These daydreams alternated with other daydreams in which Ignatius did great deeds of valor as a knight and warrior to win the favor of a great lady. He enjoyed both sets of daydreams, and for a long time did not notice that they had different emotional effects after he finished them. When he finished the dreams of doing great deeds as a warrior, he says, "he found that he was dry and unhappy." But when he finished the dreams of doing great things for Christ, "he remained happy and joyful." Then he goes on to say:

> He did not consider nor did he stop to examine this difference until one day his eyes were partially opened and he began to wonder at this difference and to reflect upon it. From experience he knew that some thoughts left him sad while others made him happy, and little by little he came to perceive the different spirits that were moving him; one

coming from the devil, the other coming from God. (*A Pilgrim's Journey: The Autobiography of Ignatius of Loyola*, by Joseph N. Tylenda.)

This story may take some of the mystery out of the process of the discernment of spirits. First of all, the interior movements Ignatius speaks of are the ordinary ones we experience all the time, happiness and joy versus sadness and dryness. Secondly, Ignatius finally paid attention to the difference in his emotional life caused by these two sets of daydreams. Thirdly, Ignatius came to the conclusion that these different emotional states resulted from thoughts and dreams caused on the one hand by God and on the other by the devil. In his rules for discernment of spirits he does not attribute all interior movements contrary to God's intentions to the devil; they can also come from our own resistance to the call of God. The main point to get from the story is that paying attention to the different emotional states caused in us by thoughts, dreams, contemplations and actions can help us to decide what God is communicating to us and what is not from God. That is what discernment of spirits is all about.

The first rule of thumb I suggest is that you look at your ordinary orientation with regard to God and to your life as a Christian. Do you try to lead a good Christian life insofar as possible? Or are you someone who cuts corners with regard to your Christian life? As an example of the latter, think of a landlord who gouges his tenants and provides few services to make their living even halfway decent. Suppose that he were to try to engage in a retreat of the kind proposed in this book. What do you think would happen in his prayer periods? Probably he would begin to feel the pangs of conscience as he begins to realize how good God has been to him. He might also feel some relief from these pangs of conscience when he had thoughts like these:

"These tenants are a lazy lot anyway; at least I'm giving them a roof over their heads." Ignatius would say that the pangs of conscience come from God and that the rationalizations that give relief come from the evil spirit or from his own unwillingness to change his life-style.

What about the person who is trying to live a decent Christian life even if not perfectly, say a working mother and wife who tries her best to do an honest day's work and to take care of her family obligations? When she begins a retreat like this, she might feel great joy and peace and look forward to the periods of prayer. Then she might experience some anxieties, feeling that she was being too proud to expect God to speak to her, or that taking time for prayer like this was a luxury she could ill afford. I remember a woman who had three very moving and wonderful days of prayer on a retreat who suddenly had the thought, "This is too high-falutin' for the likes of me." As a result her prayer became dry and boring until she realized that fear of too much closeness to God had produced the disturbing thought. Ignatius would say that in a case like this the positive experiences come from God or the good spirit who wants to make everything easy for her and that the troubling thoughts come from the bad spirit or from her fears of closeness to God.

So the first rule of thumb urges you to establish the general orientation of your life. If you are not in tune with God in your life, you can expect that God will try to get you to change your life; you will feel pangs of conscience about your life. These pangs of conscience, however, will not lead to anxious, scrupulous examinations of all your motivation; they will gently point out where you have gone wrong. The bad spirit, or your own desire not to change your life, will try to whisper blandishments in your ear to convince you that all is O.K. On the other hand, if you are trying to live in tune with God's intention, God will console you, help you to move forward, encourage you in your efforts to live a good life. But the bad spirit, or your own fear of closeness to God, will try to make you leery of developing a closer relationship with God. For example, Ignatius had the thought at one point during his retreat at Manresa: "And how will you be able to put up with this (namely his ascetical life and prayers) for the seventy years you have ahead of you?" Ignatius quite rightly answered that no one could guarantee that he would live for even one more day. The great temptation of an alcoholic is to imagine the many years of sobriety he or she will have to endure; hence the advice of the A.A. program to take one day at a time.

The second rule of thumb follows from the first. God wants us to be happy and fulfilled. But the only way we can be happy and fulfilled is to be in tune with God's desire for the world and for us. For those who are trying to lead a life in tune with God's intention, consolation is the order of the day for the most part. This does not mean that life will be without pain and suffering; it means that God wants to be a consoling presence to us even in the inevitable pains and sufferings life has in store. If this is true, then the terrible mental agony and torture scrupulous people go through is not from God. After all, scrupulous people are trying to live in tune with God. Ignatius himself, during his early days in Manresa, was plagued by scruples, fearing that he had not confessed all his sins. Things got so bad that he contemplated suicide. But at this point in his life he was trying with great fervor, indeed excessive fervor, to live his life in accordance with God's intention. He finally came to the conclusion that these scrupulous thoughts could not be from God.

As a result of these two rules of thumb, we can define spiritual consolation and spiritual desolation along Ignatian lines. Spiritual consolation is, obviously, something positive that is experienced. The word "spiritual" does not mean that the consolation goes on in us without our awareness. Spiritual consolation refers to any experience of desire for God, of distaste for one's past sins, of sympathy for Jesus or for any other suffering person. It refers, in other words, to "every increase in hope, faith, and charity, and every interior joy which calls and attracts one toward heavenly things and to the salvation of one's soul, by bringing it tranquility and peace in its Creator and Lord" (Sp. Ex. n. 316). The epistle to the Galatians lists the fruit of the Spirit as "love, joy, peace, patience, kindness, generosity, faithfulness, gentleness, and self-control" (Gal 5: 22–23). When you experience this group of movements in your being, you can be relatively sure that you are being moved by God.

Spiritual desolation is the contrary of spiritual consolation. Ignatius gives these examples:

> obtuseness of soul, turmoil within it, an impulsive motion toward low and earthly things, or disquiet from various agitations and temptations. These move one toward lack of faith and leave one without hope and without love. One is completely listless, tepid, and unhappy, and feels separated from our Creator and Lord (n. 317).

Provided that we are trying to live a good life, the experiences of feeling out of sorts, ill at ease, anxious, unhappy, listless, etc., are experiences of spiritual desolation. They do not come from God.

These definitions lead to our third rule of thumb. When we are experiencing spiritual desolation, it is not a good time to make any major decisions about our life's course. Rather, we should beg God for patience and for some light as to the causes of the desolation. We might look back to the last time when we experienced consolation and then try to examine what might have led to the desolation.

Sometimes we will discover that the desolation appeared when we became afraid of some new step forward in our relationship with God or of some change of direction in our life that seemed to be demanded if we were to remain true to ourselves and to God. For example, I might notice that desolation began when I saw Jesus forgive Peter and thought, with repugnance, about forgiving someone who had injured me. After that I avoided thinking about Jesus and Peter. But we also need to remind ourselves that we often cannot figure out the source of our desolation; no one experiences a steady diet of consolation; then we beg God for help to endure the desolation until consolation returns, as it will.

The fourth rule of thumb has to do with times of consolation. In times of consolation remember to be grateful to God for this gift. It is undeserved. You are happy because God has been good enough to draw you to a deeper union and to living out God's intention for you.

The fifth and final rule of thumb is to be open and honest with your spiritual director or with your peer group about what is actually going on in you as you try to pray. Such openness will keep you from remaining long in desolation or in false consolation. By false consolation I mean a kind of euphoria that does not conform to what is actually going on in your life. An example: a person who feels no sadness at all at the loss of a loved one, but only joy that the loved one is "in heaven." Another: a married man in his late forties who finds "new life" and "great peace" in a fundamentalist church group which estranges him from his wife, his family and his friends. Another: a religious brother who becomes greatly enthused about becoming a missionary in Brazil, but has no talent for learning languages and, in fact, is greatly needed in his present apostolate.

APPENDIX C
SELECT BIBLIOGRAPHY

A. WORKS CITED IN THIS BOOK:

Barry, William A., *God and You: Prayer as a Personal Relationship*. Mahwah, NJ: Paulist, 1987. (Also Pasay City, Philippines: Daughters of St. Paul, 1991.)

Bernanos, Georges, *The Diary of a Country Priest*. Tr. Pamela Morris. New York: McMillan, 1937, 1965.

Buechner, Frederick, *The Alphabet of Grace*. San Francisco: Harper, 1970.

Buechner, Frederick, *Lion Country*. San Francisco: Harper & Row, 1984.

Moore, Brian, *Blackrobe*. New York: Dutton, 1985.

Moore, Sebastian, *Let This Mind Be In You: The Quest for Identity through Oedipus to Christ*. San Francisco: Harper & Row/Seabury, 1985.

Tolkien, J.R.R., *The Tolkien Reader*. New York: Ballantine, 1966.

Tylenda, Joseph N., *A Pilgrim's Journey: The Autobiography
of Ignatius of Loyola*. Wilmington, DE: Michael
Glazier,   1985.

B. OTHER BOOKS THAT MIGHT BE
   HELPFUL FOR PRAYER:

Barry, William A., *"Seek My Face:" Prayer as a Personal
Relationship in Scripture*. Mahwah, NJ: Paulist, 1989.
(Also Pasay City, Philippines: Daughters of St. Paul,
1991.) Scripture passages are used to illustrate various aspects of prayer as a personal relationship.

Barry, William A., *Finding God in All Things: A Companion
to the Spiritual Exercises of St. Ignatius*. Notre Dame,
IN: Ave Maria, 1991. A description of the various
phases of the Spiritual Exercises.

Barry, William A., *God's Passionate Desire and Our Response*.
Notre Dame, IN: Ave Maria, 1993. A series of meditations that might lead to prayer.

Carmody, John, *The Quiet Imperative: Meditations on Justice
and Peace Based on Readings from the New Testament*.
Nashville, TN: The Upper Room, 1986. Each chapter
gives a text to ponder and then a meditation based
on the text.

Carmody, John, *Like an Ever-Flowing Stream: Meditations on
Justice and Peace Based on Readings from the Old
Testament*. Nashville, TN: The Upper Room, 1987.
The same format.

Dunne, Tad, *Spiritual Exercises for Today: A Contemporary
Presentation of the Classic Spiritual Exercises of Ignatius*

Loyola. San Francisco: Harper, 1991. Presents the step-by-step procession of the Spiritual Exercises to anyone who wants to make a major life choice.

Reiser, William, *Talking about Jesus Today: An Introduction to the Story behind Our Faith*. New York/Mahwah: Paulist, 1993. Takes the reader through the story of Jesus in an imaginative, highly personal way.

Tetlow, Joseph, *Choosing Christ in the World: Directing the Spiritual Exercises of St. Ignatius Loyola According to Annotations Eighteen and Nineteen. A Handbook*. St. Louis, MO: Institute of Jesuit Sources, 1989. A handbook for directors in loose-leaf form with pages to be given to those who make the Exercises.